Advance Praise for *Cash And Control*:

"Stefania's wisdom is invaluable to any entrepreneur with a big vision for his or her future."

—Dan Sullivan, Founder and President,
The Strategic Coach, Inc.

"If more entrepreneurs took advantage of the process detailed in Cash And Control, they would liberate the business visionary within and venture capitalists would gladly follow."

—Alan Patricof, Co-founder,
Apax Partners

"Stefania Aulicino combines a classic University of Chicago insight—that financial capital is in ready supply relative to entrepreneurially-oriented human capital—with practical advice to entrepreneurs who want to maintain control of the enterprises they create."

—Edward A. Snyder, Dean and
George Pratt Shultz Professor of Economics,
University of Chicago Graduate School of Business

"For much of her very active business career Stefania Aulicino has been closely involved with the process of connecting the financial and strategic sides of entrepreneurship and business building. She has collected many of the insights she has derived from this considerable experience in this book that many business builders are sure to find interesting and thought provoking."

—John P. Gould, Steven G. Rothmeier Professor and
Distinguished Service Professor of Economics,
University of Chicago Graduate School of Business

November 2005

Cash And Control:
You Can Have Both

An unconventional process for
finding money to grow your business

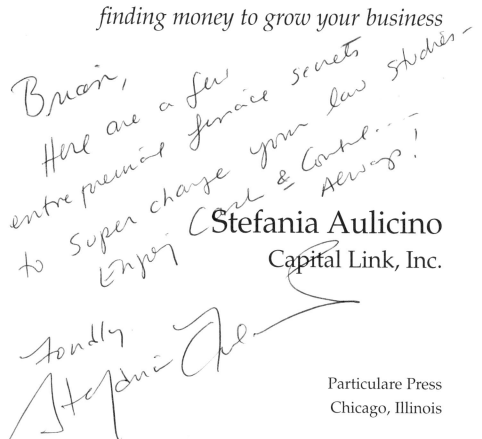

Brian,
Here are a few secrets
entrepreneurial finance
to super charge your law studies —
Enjoy Cash & Control...
Always!

Stefania Aulicino
Capital Link, Inc.

Fondly
Stefania Aulicino

Particulare Press
Chicago, Illinois

Particulare Press
Chicago, Illinois
www.ParticularePress.com

Disclaimer: This book is designed to provide accurate and
authoritative information in regard to the subject matter covered. It is
sold with the understanding that the author and publisher are not
engaged in rendering legal, tax or other professional service. Laws
vary from state to state, and if legal advice or other expert assistance is
required, the services of a competent professional should be sought.
Consequently, the author and publisher specifically disclaim any
liability, loss or risk, personal or otherwise, which is incurred as a
consequence, directly or indirectly, of the use and application of any of
the contents of this book.

ISBN # 0-9762320-0-6

Library of Congress Control Number: 2004116855

Library of Congress Cataloging-in-Production Data has been filed for.

Selected **Service Marks** of Capital Link and Capital Link USA include:

> The Entrepreneur's Advocate
> Cash And Control: You Can Have Both
> The Growth Catalyst System
> The Mosaic Approach
> The Back Door Approach
> YOU, the Business Builder—Not Funding—are the
>   Scarce Commodity.
> YOU, the Business Builder: The Most Advanced Species
>   on the Planet.
> Growth is Your Own Unique Currency.
> Vision Attracts Capital.

With appreciation for my parents and teachers *before* me,
my husband, family, and clients on this journey *with* me.

This book is dedicated to Business Builders *after* me—YOU,
who are willing to work toward your greatest vision.

STOP! IS THIS BOOK *REALLY* FOR YOU?

Entrepreneurs in the world come in all types. Just as I have come to realize that all CEOs are not entrepreneurs, I've learned that all entrepreneurs don't have the same ambitions for their businesses. Entrepreneurs, almost unwittingly, start with the end in mind; their ambition runs the spectrum from "lifestyle" at one extreme to "market leader" at the other. A lifestyle entrepreneur focuses on a way of living. A market leader, on the other hand, tirelessly strives to be the best in a chosen niche.

Entrepreneurs have long been associated with bootstrapping, an approach worn by many as a badge of entrepreneurship. Perhaps lifestyle and small-vision entrepreneurs can get away with it. But if you strive to achieve your full potential by becoming a market leader, then bootstrapping just won't do.

While many books tell you how to start or fund a small business, none directly addresses how to go beyond—how to grow a business that's already met with success yet its greatest potential still lies ahead.

Are You an Entrepreneur or a Business Builder?

As used in this book, the word "entrepreneur" means someone who limits his or her vision while a Business Builder is driven by a big, unlimited vision.

From this point forward, we leave behind the issues of the lifestyle and small-vision entrepreneurs, yielding to the pressing needs of a Business Builder—you.

Anyone can *start* a business. It takes a Business Builder to *grow* a company that's capable of *sustained profit* over time.

It begins with a simple mind shift.

Are you an Entrepreneur or a Business Builder?

Introducing You to The Entrepreneur's Advocate

This book synthesizes lessons I've learned over my 30-year entrepreneurial career—half of that as a business owner making the usual kind of entrepreneurial mistakes and the other half on Wall Street learning the business of finance from the inside out. As a real-world entrepreneur with stock market and venture community experience, I offer a unique "insider" perspective and a can-do attitude as a passionate peer. I share my knowledge of financial markets and business forces to empower fellow Business Builders to realize a future that's bigger and safer than they ever thought possible.

After a 15-year sojourn through the nation's largest financial institutions and the venture capital community, I founded my third company, Capital Link, in 1988. Capital Link puts my Wall Street "insider knowledge" to work serving big-vision entrepreneurs—the Business Builders. As THE ENTREPRENEUR'S ADVOCATE, I apply my unconventional approach for finding money to help you grow your business. This role leads me to wear many hats: a coach, catalyst, teacher, translator and more. But I'm always an advocate who delivers the right resources for your optimum growth strategy.

Insights from the distinctive perspective of *your* Advocate.

I am here to share that distinctive vantage point with you—one Business Builder to another!

Information you will find in this book could not be revealed by typical entrepreneurs, not even those who had started several companies. Why? Because such an entrepreneur would only have his or her own experiences to call upon. Nor could this information have been delivered by non-entrepreneurs like CPAs, attorneys, bankers, or investment bankers who necessarily see the world through different lenses than entrepreneurs do.

I have learned how to tap into the uniqueness of each company with which I've had the privilege to work. As a result, I've developed a process that allows me to assist growth companies to access their own genius and the unique currency they've created. This methodical process, which is called *THE GROWTH CATALYST SYSTEM*, enables you to optimize your company's growth strategy.

As your Advocate, I share hard-earned insights and contrast them to conventional wisdom throughout this book. All too often, conventional wisdom is made up of self-limiting beliefs that hold entrepreneurs back from their greatness. This book reveals profit-liberating insights from real-world situations that illustrate how The Growth Catalyst System works to uncover and fund your *OPTIMUM GROWTH STRATEGY*.

The ideas in this book challenge your thinking about the growth process. When you follow it from start to finish, you will have an action plan that brings in more than the cash you thought you needed yet keeps you in control.

My passion is to liberate the Business Builder within you—to help you harness the extraordinary energy of your vision so you can convert your business's growth potential into profitable reality. My own vision is this: *Business Builders achieve extraordinary results by design* and leave the age-old model of hard work, luck, and chance in their dust.

Stefania Aulicino
January, 2005
Chicago, Illinois
Stefania@CapitalLinkUSA.com

Cash And Control: You Can Have Both

An unconventional process for
finding money to grow your business

Table of Contents

You

Liberating the Business Builder Within

L ike all entrepreneurs, Greg had a vision. But something happened on his way to implementing his vision. His dream changed from bringing in $25 million in revenue over three years to $25 million in one year!

What happened? Greg acquired a new perception of his own company. His business had grown from $2.7 million to $7.8 million with one plant, using only internally generated funds. Yet in a single year, revenues increased from $7.8 million to $25 million with four plants in operation.

Compared with Greg's initial vision, these results are striking! So striking that he wrote the following prose and sent it to me. It expresses how his thinking about access to resources had blocked his potential:

> *I thought I knew what I had*
> > *I didn't*
>
> *I perceived attracting resources for my growth would be hard*
> > *It wasn't*
>
> *I thought I'd hate the process and the people*
> > *I didn't*
> > *I developed a network and friends*
>
> *I thought I'd hate sharing my company*
> > *Now I can't wait to share more of an even bigger company*
>
> *I thought you plan, execute, and then accept what you are offered*
> > *I discovered I had choices*
>
> *. . . and control!*
>
> > > *Greg*

Looking Forward

I am thrilled to address you, Greg, and fellow members of the economic elite: You have demonstrated proficiency in the alchemy of entrepreneurship by creating a future that did not exist—until you made it real.

Because you have already accomplished so much, you have more at stake today than ever before. That's why it's obvious you are reading this book; talented entrepreneurs always look forward, not backward.

Entrepreneurs are the heroes of America's powerful economy. Look at the evidence:

- 23 million small business owners generate 50% of the nation's Gross Domestic Product.

- Small business entrepreneurs create two out of every three new jobs.

- Small businesses represent more than 99% of all employers, employing more than half the private work force.

However, even in America, which has a high rate of success, talented and motivated entrepreneurs aren't achieving their full growth and profit potential. It's not because of the markets or the economy, but because they're relegated to *practice on themselves*. As a result, too much precious entrepreneurial energy is being wasted.

Are you pursuing your Optimum Growth Strategy?

There's no question about the amount of energy you are investing in your company. The real questions are these: "Are you pursuing The Optimum Growth Strategy for your business? Considering the investment of your time, energy, and intellectual capital, are you sure you're getting the highest ROI possible?"

Determine who's in control of your company's future. Some people say the marketplace. Some say investors. Some say fate. But not many people point to themselves and say, "Me. I'm in control of my company's future." This book supplies the ammunition to fuel that mindset.

Build a Better Future

Now it's time for you to achieve the future you *really* want as a Business Builder. It's not like becoming a CPA or MD that requires earning a degree; it's not even like being a CEO, which is a title bestowed from the outside.

Being a Business Builder comes from within *you*. It takes a commitment to create a future that wouldn't exist unless you made it so. Perhaps it starts with a reminder from a fellow Business Builder that Business Building is a high and noble calling.

Yet, sometimes it's hard to think this way because the world holds up a lot of limiting beliefs about Business Builders—beliefs that challenge the essence of what makes entrepreneurship even possible. A few of them are:

- You are being too risky!
- You are not realistic!
- You are pushing too far, too fast!
- You are going to fail!

But notice where most of that feedback comes from. Non-Business Builders. Successful Business Builders know we are not risk takers; we are risk managers. We are not unrealistic; we just see a different reality. (For example, Business Builders could "see" fax machines and cell phones before manufacturers ever made them.) We never fail without gaining something; we're simply *practicing* as we walk the path to success.

Similarly, that's both the challenge and the genius of you, the Business Builder. You persevere against criticism, even failure. You bring forth the courage to innovate, time and time again.

You move the *promise* of the future into the present.

That's what it takes to succeed in today's challenging world economy—an economy radically different from yesterday's.

Adapt to Increased Size and Pace

No, the principles of business success have not changed, but the game board has. The size of the playing field has expanded. So has the pace at which the game is now played. Due to globalization, the rate of success—or failure—has accelerated. Added to that is the fact that we live in internet time. The confluence of these two factors—size and pace—results in a phenomenal degree of uncertainty and volatility. But on the positive side, the scope of possibilities has increased exponentially. **In today's world, *innovation drives success.***

Innovation as an economic prerequisite in today's world makes your skill-set perfect because you're already well practiced in operating under uncertainty and you know how to adapt to the fast pace of change. That puts you in the driver's seat to capitalize on everything today's business world offers.

Finances Must Follow Strategy

Although business strategy and financing strategy are interrelated, letting how you finance your company dictate your future possibilities is wrong; doing so constrains you to remain a small business. The secret of successful Business Builders is to let business strategy dictate your financing needs, *never the reverse*. Herein lies the dilemma; Business Builders need financial resources.

The principles behind *Cash And Control: You Can Have Both!* are built on this pivotal, seminal revelation: *The growth potential inherent in your business strategy can be used to create a unique currency that allows you, a creative Business Builder, to access all the resources (money and people) you need and still maintain control.* (Given that many entrepreneurs have trouble securing resources, I know I must address unbelievers and I will as we proceed through this book.)

> **Your business strategy must dictate your finance strategy, never the reverse.**

This book provides an unconventional process that can make you resource-abundant without losing control to those who finance your optimum growth strategy. The payoff for applying this process—The Growth Catalyst System—is simple: You'll gain confidence to convert your growth potential into profitable reality.

When you apply this process, you'll also benefit from:

- **Exponentially higher profits by harnessing the energy you're already investing**
- **Dramatically lower risks as you accelerate growth that's built upon your strengths**

- **Enhanced shareholder wealth as you maintain control over your destiny, even in a volatile economy**

High-performance growth rarely happens by accident. Rather, it requires a proven process that can get you from *where you are* to *where you can be*. Let me put two human faces on this through example.

> Greg is president of a labor-intensive business that produces interior trim for the trucking industry. Before he took advantage of this methodical process to capture the future he really wanted, Greg was generating $3.4 million in revenue. After following this process, his company grew to $25 million in one year's time.
>
> Dan is president of a high-tech company providing electronic components for factory automation. Before he took advantage of this methodical process to capture the future he really wanted, Dan was doing $10 million with a goal of reaching $30 million. As a result of applying the same predicable process, Dan grew his company to $100 million after just 12 months.

Now, replace the names Dan and Greg with *your* name and liberate the Business Builder within you.

Transformational Insights

From this book, you will gain practical yet transformational insights to overcome the barriers that prevent the expansion and profitability you know are possible for your company. You will:

- **learn how to attract abundant resources for your next stage of growth**
- **access the secrets of self sufficiency**

- liberate the Business Builder within you to pursue the future of your choosing; and

- maintain control!

Practical yet transformational insights from one Business Builder to another

The following chapters detail a time-tested, market-proven methodology that channels the Business Builder's own genius—*your* genius—to exceed your own greatest ambitions. You deserve a predictable process to get the biggest ROI on the time, energy, and intellectual capital you're already investing to achieve profitable growth—faster and safer. It's called the Growth Catalyst System.

> " *This Growth Catalyst System released the $100 million company that was previously hidden in my $10 million firm.* "
>
> *Dan*

Cash

*Using Visionary Growth
As Your Unique Currency*

If your company is at risk of running out of cash, this book is for you. After all, the faster you grow, the more cash is a problem. By now, you've figured out that *growth consumes cash*. It's not the kind of discovery you expected to make after doing what you *thought* was the hard part:

Business Builders know GROWTH is their solution.

- You took the leap and built your own business.
- You invested in building an infra-structure to serve your clients.
- You attracted clients to your business.

Growth, however, is the "problem" only for unenlightened entrepreneurs. For Business Builders, growth is the solution, as you will learn.

When I first met Greg and Dan, each had been turned down by his bank when seeking capital to implement a visionary growth strategy.

Greg, CEO of a labor-intensive, low-tech company, wanted to increase his plant capacity to serve a key customer. His local bank, however, turned him down, assessing the move as "imprudent."

Dan, CEO of a high tech company, invested his own net worth to develop a new product line but was thwarted when his bank penalized his company for depressed profits from the expensed R&D. Dan's bank lowered his company's credit line just at the time he intended to use it to market his new product line.

From their interactions with the bank, Greg and Dan both assumed that resources were scarce and started seeking only what cash they *thought* they could get. As a result, they were running smaller businesses than they wanted to.

How about you?

- Do you believe your company has more growth and profit potential than you currently experience?
- Do your best business opportunities—or resource constraints—dictate your business strategy?
- Are you confident that you're pursing the optimum strategy to yield the highest return on the energy and resources you are already investing?

As a fellow Business Builder, I learned a solution you need to know—one that I'm compelled to share as your Advocate and Growth Catalyst.

Visionary Growth is not just a goal. Rather, Visionary Growth allows you to create your own unique currency.

This concept surely contrasts to the self-limiting notion that growth is a problem to be solved. But let's face it—growth certainly feels like a problem when you want to attract cash for a future that doesn't exist YET!

Busy entrepreneurs dream of having a single-source solution—perhaps a flexible banker or a deep-pocket investor. That would solve a lot of problems, wouldn't it? Wrong. Finding a single-source solution would be the worst thing that could ever happen to you. Inevitably, it would come at a huge price, making you hostage to that source. It could even lead to losing control of your company.

As your Advocate and Growth Catalyst, I have one request. If you take away nothing else, please remember this: Self-sufficiency for a Business Builder requires you to rely on your own unique currency.

> **Visionary growth is your unique currency.**

The Mosaic Approach

A mosaic is a picture composed of small colorful pieces. Individually, each piece has little value until a skilled craftsperson methodically assembles them to create a piece of art. Applying the concept of a mosaic to finance requires accepting this financial fact of life: *There is no single financing solution.* The right solution is made up of pieces; the resulting "artwork" will be unique to your company.

Like creating a beautiful picture from small pieces, there's an art to financing growth that creates the greatest value and achieves the lowest cost. Why? Because different capital sources have different risk-taking appetites. For example; equity is prepared to bet on the future because if the equity investor is right, ownership allows the investor to share in the profit. Debt, on the other hand, would never take such an equity risk because a lender, such as your banker, has a cap on their return; debt only earns an interest rate.

Following that logic, financing your company cost-effectively requires dividing your financial needs into small pieces. This allows you to tap different credit sources—each according to its own risk-taking appetite.

■ **The world of business falls into 2 categories:**

NON-GROWTH COMPANIES

GROWTH COMPANIES

If yours is not a growing company, you don't need resources.

If your company is growing, you consume cash and, for that matter, everything else. Access to resources is the life blood of every growing company.

■ **For Growth companies, there are 2 categories:**

THOSE WITH ACCESS TO RESOURCES

THOSE WITHOUT ACCESS

For companies with access to resources, the sky is the limit.

For those without, the only thing between them and the blue sky is the know-how to find and access resources.

■ **For Growth companies in need of resources, there are 2 categories:**

BANKABLE

UN-BANKABLE

Bankable companies are attractive to debt, equity, and other financing tools. The capital to support their growth is within their control.

Un-bankable companies are not attractive to a wide range of credit options. Therefore, scarce finances dictate sub-optimal business strategies that further limit their financial options. This cycle becomes a self-defeating prophecy, creating artificial limits on growth and profitability.

■ **Within the entrepreneurial world, there are 2 categories:**

THOSE WHO ARE WILLING TO GIVE UP THEIR GROWTH POTENTIAL

THOSE WHO AREN'T

Those who yield to the artificial limits on their growth and profitability.

Those who interrupt the unacceptable cycle of artificial limitations and apply a fresh new approach to financing your growth and profitability.

A financing solution is available to any company committed to growth, bankable *or* un-bankable. This is because *your company's visionary growth is its own special currency.* The most cost-effective way to profit from your own unique currency is to use the *MOSAIC APPROACH*, which is built with your own resources.

This Mosaic Approach takes advantage of the principle of divide and conquer. Think of each individual fleck of color as a different resource that, all together, make up your financial solution and allow you to capitalize on the unique currency of your visionary growth.

To see how this MOSAIC APPROACH might apply to you, let's follow the steps of a savvy manager named Jack.

The Mosaic Approach takes advantage of the principle of divide and conquer.

Jack wanted to explore the power of the mosaic to finance a new product introduction and asked for my help. Based on Jack's business judgment, he had figured out the most promising growth strategy, so it was easy to calculate the expenses required to support the revenue he projected.

Jack calculated the raw materials, labor, plant, marketing, administrative, and equipment expenses he would require. All together, he needed $4 million to finance his new product introduction.

In my experience, a financial mosaic is typically composed of 6 to 12 individual pieces. Our job became identifying various mosaic pieces required to address Jack's expenses.

First, I explained to Jack that a mosaic is most valuable when it's built on creditors who stand to benefit from his company's success. I call this "cashing in" on vendor and customer relationships. Why? Because these sources are best able to lend credibility, which lowers the uncertainly of your company's future and makes it more attractive to additional resources.

So, instead of going to a lender as a first move, we focused on Jack's customer prospects. Let's face it, if Jack's new product doesn't interest his customers, it won't interest anyone else, least of all a lender.

But I encouraged Jack not to query just any customer; he identified the most highly respected industry players and made appointments with the highest corporate decision makers possible. Jack sought and received the opportunity to show the compelling economics of his new product to five industry leaders. Three of these companies wanted to place orders.

But Jack wanted more from them; he wanted cash. So I suggested Jack offer a lucrative first-time purchase price—with terms of 50% cash with order.

Although Jack couldn't believe it was possible at first, his three customers were delighted with their transaction. In this way, Jack accessed his **first** piece of the mosaic—a little bit of cash. Simultaneously, he earned a **second** piece of his mosaic—a great deal of financial market credibility.

Next, he approached vendors of parts and supplies for his new product. With customer orders in hand, it didn't take a huge selling effort to get their attention. Based on his success with three industry-respected, highly visible key customers, he had the vendors salivating as they envisioned an increasing stream of big-purchase orders. Jack simply focused their attention on the awesome size of the market and rate of growth with which he planned to penetrate it. Voilá, he had his **third** mosaic piece—vendor participation.

Frankly, with this new product, Jack offered a solution

to these vendors who were faced with unpredictable sales. Their long-standing customers weren't ordering as much as they had in years past. Other customers had actually gone out of business. These vendors dared not miss the opportunity to link up with a rising star. Consequently, two vendors immediately agreed to defer payment terms, one for three months, another for six. With these agreements, Jack's **third** mosaic piece provided him a resource outside of conventional selling terms and beyond what he'd thought possible.

> **The Mosaic Approach builds on your company's visionary growth as your own unique currency.**

For a highly aggressive twist, rather than delaying the cash expenses associated with a top-flight lawyer and accountant, Jack found and hired the most recognized specialists in his industry. In addition, he selected several highly visible professional advisors. He was counting on the "Power of Perception" to convert those advisory *fees* into cash-attracting *assets*. This outsourced intellectual capital became his **fourth** mosaic piece. Together with these advisors, we put together a package to make Jack's future tangible enough for outsiders to understand.

With these pieces of his mosaic in place, Jack has three key customers offering cash deposits, two vendors extending significant credit, an industry-recognized lawyer, a top-notch CPA, plus other highly respected advisory board members. Jack's future was now tangible enough for even those outside his industry to understand. He was ready for the big test!

Jack headed off to the banks—not one, but several banks. He shared his projections and asked the bankers what they could offer. Lo and behold, one banker did business with several of Jack's customers and was happy to advance against those receivables. Jack had found his **fifth** mosaic piece.

Using his new insight that his Visionary Growth is, in fact, his unique currency, Jack realized he could ask for a better than normal advance rate from the bank. Because this banker knew more about Jack's receivables than standard receivables they typically lend against, he got the enhanced advance rate he sought— and his **sixth** mosaic piece.

But, the real stretch came when the banker realized Jack already had these things in hand: credit support from customers and vendors the bankers knew, an auditor they trusted, and several impressive professional advisors on his team. That allowed them to feel comfortable about Jack achieving his projections. This increased comfort led Jack's new bank to offer an over-advance line, which provided breathing room— and his **seventh** mosaic piece. If Jack's new product succeeded, the new bank would ride his coattails. Remember, banks *are* in the business of lending money; giving them good reasons to lend it to you makes them look good.

However, even with all these mosaic pieces in place, Jack still fell short of raising the $4 million he needed. Fortunately, based on the enthusiastic responses he was getting, Jack had become sophisticated about dividing his financing needs into small pieces. Each piece he put in place lowered the risk to the next piece.

> In that way, he conquered a wider range of credit options because he lowered the uncertainly of his future.
>
> The effect of combining his first **seven** mosaic pieces actually created his **eighth** mosaic piece— Jack's facility in applying the "power of positive perception". Jack uncovered several more capital alternatives unique to him.

Capital alternatives might include these ideas—ones that you could possibly use:

- Barter—A non-cash banking system that uses the retail price of your product to swap for products from other members of the barter club.
- Outsourcing—In an age of specialization, outsourcing lets you take full advantage of some other company's economies of scale.
- International offset—Getting established companies to ease your entry into foreign markets, at their cost.

You see, with growth as a Business Builder's currency, creativity is the only limiting factor when selecting pieces for his financial mosaic. Now that Jack has mosaic pieces to finance all $4 million of his expenses, his financial picture looks fairly complete, doesn't it? Well, it would be if only revenues would come in exactly as Jack forecasted they should. But that never happens, does it?

Don't Forget the Timing Gap

So far in this example, Jack had only handled the Known expenses associated with growth. But what about the Unknown?

Let me explain. Whenever you introduce a new product or expand into a new market, expenses precede revenue, which results in a *Timing Gap* before expenses and revenues synchronize.

Even when prudent business people price their products to generate a profit, negative cash flow occurs during the Timing Gap before expenses and revenues synchronize.

The most difficult thing about this Timing Gap is how to finance it, because, after all, it's an Unknown. Among the greatest questions facing any growing company is just how long a new product will take to achieve market acceptance. That is, how long will the Timing Gap exist?

Equity Finances the Unknown

While you can tap into a variety of ways to finance the Known expense using the Mosaic Approach, there's only one way to finance the Unknown—and that's with equity. Equity becomes the critical safety net to ensure against the Unknowns and gives your growing company staying power.

Growth requires financing both the Known and the Unknown expenses.

If it's so simple, then why do growing companies undercapitalize themselves? Perhaps because equity is not just cash; it's linked to control. Perhaps it's because unknowing entrepreneurs have been misled to fear equity. Perhaps it's because Equity mistakenly connotes a loss of control. These misconceptions have kept many, many entrepreneurs and their companies from achieving their full growth and profit potential.

That's why financing growth is a two-step process. Fortunately, this two-step process makes equity the smallest piece with the highest value—leveraged by your financial mosaic. *As a result, no single piece of Jack's financial mosaic is responsible for his company's success, therefore he's held hostage to none!*

Which Equity is Right for You?

Some equity is smarter about your business than others; some equity has a higher "multiplier" effect because it can attract other capital; some equity can open doors and offer non-monetary contacts worth a fortune. The real question becomes which equity is right for your company?

With the Mosaic Approach, no single financial component is responsible for your success and you are hostage to none.

First, let me remind you of two things:

- Debt and equity are not substitutes for each other; they are required complements for a growing company.

- Traditional wisdom is that debt costs less than equity, but, in reality, it depends. It could be true in the vacuum of slow or stalled growth. You see, debt financing tends to be constrained by a company's historic performance projected forward and typically is limited to collateral levels today.

Now that you're willing to consider equity, where will you find it? What do you really know about it to help you get started?

Let me tell you a secret: The future you allow yourself to see defines the appropriate choice of funding for you. Only business possibilities as defined by your Optimal Growth Strategy can determine the right finance strategy for you. The result is that **when your future is dramatically bigger than your past, equity can be your cheapest form of growth funding.**

But beware that not all equity is the same; you need to determine which equity will be your cheapest form of growth capital to address your Timing Gap. And, using what you know about your unique currency, it only makes sense that you will want to uncover the private equity investor for whom that currency is *most* valuable.

Equity comes in two forms:

- Discretionary
- Committed

It also comes in three different "classes":

- Family/Friends
- Angels
- Professional investors

Equity is the cheapest form of growth funding when your future is worth more than your past.

To capitalize on their differences, be realistic about what you have to *sell* to investors. You see, different investors are attracted to different stages of growth, so different types of investors can play complementary roles as a company grows. Properly used, different investors will yield escalating valuation!

Let's discuss in detail the three classes of equity.

Equity #1: Family/Friends

An entrepreneur has a lot of clout with the class of Family/Friends. After all, would your mother turn you down for money if you really begged her for it? But friends and relatives have their limits as investors. They only invest as an exception, they only invest in people they know, and they typically invest only in small amounts. However, while this class of friends and family offers small dollars individually, they are without a doubt the most prolific investors in aggregate. After the entrepreneur's own resources, investments from Family/Friends are represented in every successful deal I have ever seen. Best of all, these investors are easy to find; you already know them all!

Family/Friends make the ideal investors at the start-up phase of a company because at this stage, it consists only of an idea. Its greatest asset is the entrepreneur; the only thing an entrepreneur has to sell is "integrity" and the will to build a business; nothing else exists yet. Who can "buy" integrity and "will" power? Only someone for whom it already exists, someone an entrepreneur already knows because integrity is only earned over time. That's why financing a start-up typically comes only from Family/Friends investors who also provide a fundamental credibility factor. Besides, if you can't get money from those who know you, why should anyone else bet on you?

When seeking investors from the ranks of Family/Friends, consider this:

- Understand that these investors are created, not found. Don't be afraid to ask Family/Friends for what you want even if they have never invested before. Be excited about sharing what you offer with those you feel close to and care about the most.

- Use your passion to articulate that vision—that's what you're selling. Apply the principles leaned in the Mosaic Approach. Your ability to communicate your vision becomes a valuable currency.

- To help protect this important relationship, consider using a debt instrument offering them a higher-than-market interest rate. Remember, often their biggest motive is to help you, not make a huge profit. In fact, some family investors are happy with just a return of their principal.

- Think broadly about who's in your circle of family and friends. Don't limit your thinking to those you're related to by blood or those you grew up with. Most of us had a career before starting a company. Consider contacting former colleagues and professionals (attorney, CPAs, etc.) you've worked with. Ask anyone who would buy into your integrity.

- You might hear that a private placement memorandum is required. But that's not true. When dealing with people you know, the use of such a legal document is often not purposeful and can create a diversion. IMPORTANT CAVEAT—*as with all investment discussions in this book, I'm not offering legal advice but rather suggestions coming from practical business experience.*

The ideal role for the class of Family/Friends equity investors is as silent investors who know and trust you because they buy your integrity.

Equity #2: Financial Angels

Next is the class of Financial Angels—experienced business-people who have enough discretionary money that they can invest a few hundred thousand dollars "as a side line" or a hobby. Angels typically invest in the range of $100,000 to several millions, but they too have their limits: Angels only invest in businesses they understand, based on their personal operating experiences. That's understandable because they're investing their own money.

Financial Angels are ideal investors when a company has a prototype/product and needs to demonstrate its market demand. In fact, when a company gets beyond the idea stage but before it demonstrates market demand, Angels **Angels** are the cheapest source of funds for initial marketing. **are made,** Because they have relevant industry and business **not born!** knowledge that helps them make their investment decisions, Angels are willing to take an entrepreneurial gamble in the face of scant evidence.

Finding Angels is not as difficult as you might think in today's environment—especially when you understand their real investment drive. Think of Angels as "unrelated" family and friends and look for them among your industry and professional contacts. Seek those who understand your industry and know you through trade associations. They could be former employers, vendors, professionals, advisors, and so on. Like you did with Family/Friends investors, once you identify potential Angels, you can convert them into investors, even if they've never invested before. Angels are made, not born!

Equity #2a: The Brain Trust

Financial Angels come in two extremes: those with more money than time, and those with more time than money. Over the years, I have attracted a resource pool of managers who have a little of both. I call this pool the Brain Trust, a group of managers with 15 to 45 years of experience in many disciplines: operations, marketing, finance, manufacturing, quality control, and more. They're experienced in all industries—high tech, low tech, service, and so on. Not only are these sophisticated managers, they are also managers willing to invest.

Brain Trust Managers offer top-notch talent without upfront cash.

What's unique about these managers is they are not looking for "jobs." Unlike typical employees who can *only* execute a strategy if you articulate it for them in great detail, Brain Trust managers share your vision and can design the strategy as well as supply the talent to get the job done.

Brain Trust managers are attracted by a company's vision, have the skills needed to get there and are also willing to invest. Brain Trust investments can take many forms: deferred compensation, below-market salaries, and/or cash in exchange for a form of participation in future success.

These Brain Trust managers are motivated not by what you already have but by the opportunity you present to build value.

They have a drive to share in a future they help create.

When the word got out I was working with Business Builders, managers like these began to contact me. Why? Because Financial Angels have as much trouble finding you as you have finding them. Every day, Brain Trust managers call my office looking for companies like yours.

So, you see, I've attracted a unique resource pool. But having a resource pool of solutions simply isn't enough. I had to create an unconventional process to match the right solutions with my clients' specific problems. That's why I reversed the flow of résumés: Instead of circulating manager résumés for Business Builders to consider, I've created a *CORPORATE RÉSUMÉ* that details their vision, strengths, and weaknesses for Brain Trust managers to consider. In this way, individual Brain Trust managers can play a proactive role *by selecting themselves* based on matched visions and talents. Understand that Brain Trust managers are *only* attracted to problems they have the skills to solve.

Let's face it. Entrepreneurs—even Business Builders—might know exactly where they want their businesses to go, but they don't always know the best way to get there. Managers, however, know how to get there; they're just not sure where they want to go—yet! So reversing the résumé flow to access the Brain Trust allows each Brain Trust manager to contribute what he or she knows best.

Mary's Experience with Brain Trust

Mary, an experienced engineer, had built her business to $1.5 million over six years. Her company sold a top-of-the-line, $1,000 custom-tailored seat cushion for people in wheelchairs—all the while competing with products selling for a few hundred dollars.

Her growth, she thought, was limited by the size of the wheelchair market and the expense of producing her proprietary high-tech solution—even though her seating systems offered dramatic therapeutic advantages. Limited by her own background, Mary had no marketing talent in-house because she believed her products sold on their engineering attributes alone.

Instead of circulating a traditional manager résumé for Mary to evaluate, I circulated the Corporate Résumé detailing Mary's vision, strengths, and weaknesses for Brain Trust managers to consider.

One Brain Trust manager named Jim had just been merged out of a company that designed medical insurance reimbursement software programs. Jim immediately zeroed in on pricing as a key competitive problem affecting Mary marketing strategy.

Jim offered to design and install a software system for Mary's existing distributors that would allow insurance reimbursement at point-of-sale. Her product price dropped from $1,000 to $200, as a result of an 80% insurance reimbursement rate. Jim even offered to defer his compensation for the opportunity to share in the value he created. Mary was delighted to find someone so creative to help attain her goals. Her sales skyrocketed.

Another Brain Trust manager named Sara contributed the critical marketing talent, plus she offered $250,000 at a valuation that reflected the benefits of Jim's value-building contribution.

Using less cash than she ever believed possible, Mary's business revenues tripled within three years.

This is just one of the creative solutions that surfaced through this unusual approach. Brain Trust managers provided Mary with solutions to resolve the business risks, which made her more attractive to investors. Brain Trust managers can offer top-notch talent without requiring cash upfront—giving you the power to resolve business risks before funding. The Brain Trust demonstrates another way of using unique currency—visionary growth when applied

---

Consider these rules of thumb as you think about equity from these sources:

- Don't offer more than 5% ownership for funds from an individual Family/Friend investor.
- Don't offer more than 10% ownership for funds from an individual Angel investor.

If those percentage guidelines surprise you, remember the power of your unique currency; your Visionary Growth. *Investors can only generate interest on their capital. It takes an entrepreneur to generate a **profit**.*

---

to Financial Angel class of investors.

Reminder:

- Financial Angels are created, not born. These individuals can use their own cash and make their own decisions based on personal knowledge of your industry.
- Angels are often found in Choirs; they know each other as peers. But don't ask them about profession-

al investment capital, which is a different "class."

- An Angel must be a glove-fit for your needs in order to drive the value that aligns with your goals.

Caveat:

- You might find some "newbie" capital. Don't let newly wealthy individuals without business experience in your industry practice on your company.

- Watch out for "cocktail advisors" who actually buy the right to tell you what to do, so they can tell friends they're advising a growing company or have a piece of it.

- Beware of group money or "institutional Angels." A new phenomenon has evolved in which a group of people get together to make investments in private companies. However, they make decisions by committee, compared with real Financial Angels who make investments based on their own evaluations. There is nothing wrong with one industry-knowledgeable Angel inviting and educating fellow Angels to come along, but that is not the same as "institutional" Angel capital in which several individual investors "hire" one to make their decision. This spawns an agent relationship—not appropriate for the most valuable Financial Angel relationship.

Because Angels, like Family/Friends, are an informal investment source, statistics about their activities are hard to come by. However, to give you an idea of their proportionate contribution, let's say Angels invest at a rate at over 20,000 deals a year in the U.S. That's still less money than all individuals as a class.

To dramatize the relative size of these funding classes, let's say that if all funds from Family/Friends totaled $100 billion, it would contrast to around $75 billion in aggregate from all Angel investors. Because both are discretionary, statistics are hard to pin down. But the concept is clear: although Angels invest in bigger chucks, in aggregate they invest far less money then all individuals as a class. And Professional investors actually invest far less

Funding need:	$1————$100,000————$1,000,000 ++		
Ideal Source:	Family	Angels	Professionals
Market Depth:	$100 billion	$75 billion	$ 35 billion

than Angels do, as this chart shows.

Most entrepreneurs stop with these first two options in their search for equity to finance their Timing Gap because:

1. Family/Friends and Angel financing is best accessed through personal connections.
2. Their goals for growing their businesses won't attract any other kind of financing—which is a shame because it means they're not using their Visionary Growth to create their own unique currency to the fullest.

If, however, you are fortunate enough to attract experienced Angels, they expect you to need more capital than they can provide for you to be really successful. If new capital doesn't come in, their Angel investment— and yours—is in danger. Unfortunately, even experienced Financial Angels are rarely the right people to help you get access to the next class of equity; attracting Professional Equity just isn't their job. In their world, knowing a handful of fellow investors is sufficient.

When you see media reports about investment capital drying up, they are frequently referring to the discretionary equity classes. Discretionary Family/Friends and Angels investors deal in small, one-shot transactions because they're limited by personal net worth that gets tapped out quickly.

Business Builders need to know how to access the Professional Equity market to fund their Visionary Growth.

Equity #3: Professional Equity

In contrast to individual investors, *committed* equity is amassed in the Professional Equity marketplace, made up of professionals who invest as a full-time job. You could think of professional investors as portfolio managers each managing the capital of their clients, insurance companies, and pension funds, and whose investment dollars are typically held in ten-year partnerships. These professional investors invest in private companies such as yours, and earn a higher rate of return than their clients can in the traditional public markets.

What attracts these professional investors? Bold plans! And they understand that their ability to deliver higher rates of returns for *their* clients depends on *your* company's success.

Professional investment firms might have several hundred million dollars under management. To put that much money to work, they typically invest several million dollars at a time. But they too have limits. They only invest in businesses they can prudently analyze; their decisions must reflect a fiduciary responsibility as agents of their clients.

A useful reference is PriceWaterhouseCoopers "MoneyTree Survey" that tracts professional investments by quarter, by industry, by geography, and by stage of deal (early, expansion, and late). (*www.pwcmoneytree.com*)

When is a good time to approach professional investors? Ideally when your product is ready for full commercialization.

Professional Equity investors are the only source that has pockets deep enough to undertake a national or global roll out with the speed necessary to protect your investment. At that point in time, you have the evidence these investors need to evaluate the economics of the deal. Remember, Professional Equity investors are only appropriate for big futures.

Professional Private Equity investors as a class have the smallest sum of capital to invest—about $35 billion dollars—managed by a handful of a few thousand investor teams. Their funds can be found in various directories, including:

1. **Infon** offers 3,496 firms, which includes private, public, corporate, and governmental venture investment groups (www.infon.com)

2. **Galante's Venture Capital & Private Equity Directory** offers 2,350 funds published by Private Equity Analyst/Dow Jones and Co. (www.assetnews.com)

3. **Pratt's Guide** has several products published by Thomson Financial/Venture Economics (www.ventureeconomics.com)

4. **National Association of Venture Capitalists** (NVCA) is a professional association of approximately 450 venture capital and private equity firms. The NVCA's mission is to foster greater understanding of the importance of venture capital to the U.S. economy, and support entrepreneurial activity and innovation. (www.nvca.org)

Unfortunately, these directories don't always differentiate between Leverage Buy Out (LBO) investors, Venture Capital investors, and Growth Equity investors. Leverage Buy Out investors want to buy 100% of a company, then give back just a sliver to management as an incentive to run the company. Early-stage Venture Capital investors take a big equity stake for a small sum of dollars because they invest in young companies and take big risks. Growth Equity investors provide big bucks for just a minority equity position. They don't want control; they want you in charge.

Selecting the right Professional Equity investor among all these players takes a professional! Unlike the class of Family/Friends and Financial Angels that you can and should approach directly, this professional marketplace requires a different approach. You're best to have an introduction to select the right professional investor because "vulture capital" results from not being prepared to enter the world of professional equity.

Most entrepreneurs have misconceptions about the percent ownership Professional Equity will seek. As a rule of thumb, let me suggest 25% for a growth company's first round of Professional Equity, knowing you'll likely need multiple rounds of funding to achieve your vision. Realize that Professional Growth Equity investors want you in control. Caution: Don't get confused by other types of Professional Equity including LBO funds and early-stage Venture Capitalist with their higher percentage ownership stake.

Finding Equity on Your Terms

I delight in educating Business Builders about the Professional Private Equity marketplace. Why? Because these Growth Equity Professional investors want you to be in control. That shouldn't be surprising once you realize this market exists for the specific purpose of funneling dollars into investments with growth-driven potential. Therefore, these professional investors realize that if management isn't motivated, their investment upside can't be assured. After all, they are investing based on the fact that your future is worth more than your past. That makes professional investors your ideal source to fund your Visionary Growth.

Let me put this in perspective. When growth is your dilemma, there are not many alternative capital sources where you can get credit for your future. Most creditors, like your banker, extrapolate from past performance. Most investors, as evident in the public stock market, put a lot of emphasis on the last buy/sell order. In contrast, the Professional Private Equity market invests based only on your future.

This progressive growth financing attitude is not benevolent— it's the result of the structure of this market. The Professional Private Equity market is funded by institutions and pension funds that commit dollars

Growth Equity Professionals want YOU in control!

for growth investment into ten-year partnerships managed by professional growth investors. That's probably why they call it the professional private equity market. As you might guess, a manager in a partnership with a ten-year horizon can be mighty patient— but that risk tolerance changes over time. With new ten-year partnerships having been funded every year now for more than a decade, we now have portfolios of varying age (which was not true when the Professional Private Equity market was very young).

Today, those different time horizons accommodate companies at different stages of growth. Let me explain it this way: A partnership with seven years left has enough of a time horizon to invest in companies commercializing new products, like those of you who have new product plans. A different partnership with five years left will be interested in established companies that are planning aggressive expansion, like those of you with market expansion plans that can show near-term results. A partnership with only few years left of its ten-year life cycle invests in more mature situations, Leverage Buy Outs (LBO), for example. In reality, professional partnerships today focus on investing all their committed capital in just the first three to four years of their fund's life in order to raise another round of capital (called a follow-on fund). But the concept above still applies.

Another attribute of the Professional Private Equity market is its deep pockets. Growth capital must be committed capital. It creates a mismatch to undertake a multi-year growth program with uncommitted dollars. Committed investors have committed investment dollars. In additional to an initial investment, these investors set aside follow-up capital at the same time they make the original investment. Discretionary investors, on the other hand, are hard to get a commitment from because their investment dollars are here today, gone tomorrow. Discretionary dollars are subject to a prior call to fix a leaky roof or satisfy an urge for a last-minute vacation. (More detail about the Professional Equity market is in Chapter 5—Control.)

There are plenty of committed dollars around, if you know where to look. Recently, this market attracted a bubble of investment funneled into ten-year partnerships: 2000 was a peek year in which the Professional Private Equity Market raised $182 billion, in contrast to $35.6 billion raised just one year earlier, all committed to ten-year partnerships. Today, more than $35 billion of new institutional growth equity is under management. As a result, more than 2,000 partnerships are competing aggressively for companies like yours. That makes Professional Private Equity investors like money managers who have large capital portfolios to invest.

Do you have any idea how tough it is to be a money manager in the cash surplus environment we have today? To differentiate themselves, many partnerships have specialized by industry and operate as niche players. From your perspective, that means this Professional Private Equity market represents a source in which *all capital is not the same*. In this market today, more than ever before, there are:

- more growth dollars
- investing in more industries, at
- more stages of growth.

Understanding the differences among private (not public[1]) Equity investors allows you to divide your investment needs so you can benefit from escalating valuation with each round of funding. Remember:

- Family/Friends are willing to invest cheap, even when you don't have much evidence.
- Financial Angels are willing to value your company for future possibility, not for what exists now.
- Professional investors can only value what they can document.

Investors Do Think Alike

Even though you can approach different types of investors (Family/Friends, Angels, and Professional Equity), don't lose sight of the fact that investors think exactly alike.

All investors want to make money; none wants to lose principal; none wants to invest in a management team that aims to lose money. That's not to say growth investors don't expect some

---

1 *"Public" refers to what the masses want to buy on the public exchange. If you want to access these funds, you need to be ready when the public market is open. But going public isn't necessary for the money, given the depth of the private equity market. However, the public market could be an excellent exit for your company, if and when you're ready to use it that way.*

losses, but they expect losses as a risk of dealing with the uncertainty of the future. It's one thing to work around events the Business Builder can't control; it's another thing planning to be out of control by projecting several years of losses.

Investors want to invest in people who manage risk and think big! They're known to complain about a "dearth of quality deals." Most people would prefer to invest in an opportunity to build a $100 million business rather than a "nice" $20 million business.

Selecting the *right* investor is determined by who *you* are and what kind of company you intend to build. Ambition and growth stage aren't the only factors affecting your selection. Another factor is the market your business serves. Companies cater to small, static market niches at one extreme or rapidly growing billion-dollar markets at the other, with hundreds of variations in between. Small static markets generate limited returns, even with premium pricing. Conversely, markets with unconstrained growth offer unlimited profit opportunities. Professional investors like big markets to protect their big investments because big markets allow for mistakes, with built-in room to recover.

Regard selecting an Equity investor like getting married. A good relationship is synergistic; a bad one disastrous!

Just as you want more than money, professional investors want to invest more than cash. When selecting a Professional Equity Investor, you're smart to seek a smart-money Equity partner who's willing and able to fuel your Business Building vision.

But to get the best deals on Professional Equity, you need to learn more about cash and control, and an Advocate to guide you—so keep reading. But for now, here are your key takeaways about Equity:

- The best growth investors are "created, not found."
- Best investors are willing to offer more than money—smart money provides contacts and ideas to propel you and your vision forward.

- Family/Friends and Financial Angels are equity classes you can approach directly, but you need a professional to capitalize on the Professional Equity class.
- Just as with the Mosaic Approach, YOU are in control—when you know your options.

If you have growth in your marketplace, now is the ideal time to share your ambitions with those who could benefit. Mosaics are waiting to be built!

Like Jack, Greg, and Dan discovered:

- Visionary Growth was their unique currency.
- The Mosaic Approach gave them assurance against their greatest fear: loss of control.
- Equity is a Safety Net.

That's when they became energized about building the future they really wanted.

Do What You Do Best

In the entrepreneurial world are two kinds of entrepreneurs: those who are part of the solution and those who are part of the problem. You, the entrepreneur, are your company's most valuable asset—on or off the balance sheet. Conversely, you dilute your company's value every time you divert your attention from what you do best.

Mosaics are waiting to be built!

Successful entrepreneurs learn to leverage themselves by focusing exclusively on what they do best, and surrounding themselves with other experts who share their vision and goals. For you, that means enrolling customers and vendors who support your ambitions, selecting advisors who can offer perspective, and attracting managers who will make it all happen. This also means not being afraid to seek deep-pocketed investors who will help you bring your future into the present.

Growth only flourishes where there are believers. The challenge of growth is to build a team, inside and out, that's dedicated to what your company could be. The next step is YOURS!

So what future do YOU really want?

Chapter 3

Clarity

Uncovering Your Optimum Growth Strategy

Are you crystal clear about which future to pursue? What is your company's Optimum Growth Strategy?

Whenever I ask that question, I'm usually met with blank stares. I discovered that even Business Builders have difficulty speaking in terms of their _optimum_ future.

The problem is operating from a belief system that channels your thinking unconsciously.

To peer beyond your company's current horizon, it's best to discard anything that obscures your Optimum Growth Strategy from view. What is obscuring your view? Probably all these unchallenged assumptions that have artificially limited your potential for success.

Here's the dilemma: Pondering your Optimum Growth Strategy entails BIG thinking, visionary thinking, thinking from the top down. But at the moment, you're worried about mundane, short-term hassles. You're thinking from the bottom up.

Well, I have great news for you: You've just won the lottery. And its payoff has reached at an all-time high! _Now_ you have unlimited resources with which to grow your company. _Now_ you can think BIG. _Now_ you can implement your visionary growth strategy. *Now* you're thinking from the top down.

Go ahead and discard the assumptions that used to hold you back—ones like these:

- Growth capital is scarce.
- Growth capital is expensive.
- The cost of growth capital is control.
- You're not yet ready for explosive growth.
- Now is not the time.

With your windfall of unlimited resources, your company looks a lot different, doesn't it? A lot bigger. It's suddenly a lot more fun, too, isn't it?

Okay, come back to reality. You haven't won the lottery (sorry!) but the idea of winning it helps you separate business *possibilities* from financial *assumptions* that have artificially limited your potential for success. This is a seminal step toward moving the promise of your future into the present.

Think Big!

Knowing that you have all the funding necessary to eliminate impediments to your success, what amazing business milestones or goals have you envisioned? How many locations do you have? How many employees do you have here? Worldwide? What revenue level and profit margins are you achieving? Don't limit your thinking to only 12 months, and not even five years. Stretch out into the future. Based on unlimited resources, what is your company capable of achieving?

What if resources were unlimited, as if you had just won the lottery?

What future will you let yourself see passionately and freely? Liberate the visionary Business Builder within you.

Maybe you've dreamed about building your business with

unlimited resources or even joked about it. But have you ever shared this picture with your company's management staff, discussed it with your CEO or other peer group, Board of Directors, or professional advisors—even your spouse?

I bet the answer is no. This picture is just too damn big, too scary! Besides that, growth consumes cash. And we live in a world where resources have limitations.

For you, the Business Builder, to start this discussion, ask yourself: What are the three biggest opportunities you'd like to capture within the next 12 to 18 months?

Working with ambitious privately owned companies every day, I find their top three opportunities fall into these few categories. Let's see if it's true for you. Will you:

- Expand into new geographic or customer markets?
- Introduce new products?
- Invest in additional technology?
- Increase existing capacity?

Great. Now, what are the three most significant strengths your firm has to build on and capture those opportunities? I've noticed strength also seems to fall into a few categories. Will you build on:

- The excellence of your team/management?
- Loyal and repeat customers?
- Your company's excellent reputation in the marketplace?
- Proprietary and/or highly efficacious products/services?

Well then, what's holding you back from achieving your company's full potential? What are your key obstacles? From constantly interacting with Business Builders, I uncovered these top obstacles and secret fears:

- Insufficient resources to capture new opportunities
- Not enough information to make confident decisions
- Fear of making the wrong decision
- Lack of clarity about *which* future to pursue
- Fear of losing control

All business owners know that business strategy and financing strategy are interrelated. Unfortunately, most link them in the wrong sequence. Conventional wisdom declares that the availability of resources dictates business strategy. As an entrepreneur, are you willing to let bankers and bean counters set your priorities about what opportunities you'll pursue?

Business strategies dictate finance strategies, *never* the reverse!

Liberating yourself from a scarce-resource mindset is difficult. Scarcity thinking becomes so ingrained that it's easy to believe these financial constraints are real. Old habits—and fears—die slowly! So it was with Greg:

> Greg had grown his company with internally generated funds by squeezing increased productivity out of a single plant. He knew he had more demand from his customers and he wanted to build capacity to take advantage of it. But, like a lot of entrepreneurs, Greg fell into a trap.
>
> Several years before, he had been turned down by representatives at his bank and several other financial institutions for the $1 million he needed to build new capacity for his $3.5 million company. After getting turned down, he formed an assumption that resources were scarce. At some point, he stopped asking for what he really wanted and started asking

> for what he thought he could get.
>
> Ever since that happened, Greg designed his company's entire future based on limited resources—without ever questioning his assumption. (The same thing happened to Dan, but we'll get back to him later).

Sound familiar? For a Business Builder, assumptions like that are catastrophic! Remember, your vision—your ability to build a much bigger future—is your most salable asset. If you just allow it to, that vision liberates capital! Here's how Greg's vision was reinvigorated:

> Greg was surprised by my initial questions in our discussion about why he wanted $ 1 million. "What if you could have more than one plant, how would your business plan change? How would you build your business to achieve its full potential? Alternatively, what revenue level would your company be capable of based on unlimited resources?"
>
> Sitting straight up in his chair, Greg said "$100 million." Hearing himself say that, he looked a little surprised. Then he reverted to his old posture, almost taking back his words. You see, even though Greg had an intuitive sense he could achieve $100 million in revenue, he didn't believe the resources were available. He'd never exercised the muscles needed to create a $100 million company because he didn't understand that vision liberates capital—millions and millions and millions of dollars of capital.

With new confidence that he could have both cash and control, Greg got excited about taking action—but was unclear about how to proceed. He hadn't exercised the muscles necessary to let his company's best opportunities determine *which* future would be right.

While growth companies must embrace fast moving opportunities, not all growth will yield high performance results for your company. So how do you know what's your Optimum Growth Strategy?

Vision liberates capital.

First, understand that growth is safest when you build on your uniqueness. That uniqueness depends on what your company does best, and what business you're really in. The longer you've been in business, the harder that question becomes. And for a fast-growth company, the answer is a moving target!

To have safe, ever-increasing profits, I suggest identifying and building your Optimum Growth Strategy on your company's COMPETITIVE ECONOMIC DISTINCTION. Your Competitive Economic Distinction defines how you uniquely deliver value for your clients.

The Team Discovery Process

So let's get practical. Involve your team in finding answers to your questions. While setting the course for your company's future is clearly the responsibility of the CEO, no skipper would navigate his boat on the changing seas without input from his crew. Take the time to check in with your senior management team.

Here's why. Often, CEOs move so rapidly that their teams—charged with execution—don't stay on the courses their leaders have charted. Worse, these CEOs don't have input from the field to influence the course—creating what I call the Vision Gap. When the Vision Gap is eliminated, it makes room for powerful Vision-Driven Growth to takes place.

I have discovered the best way to address the question of "what business are you really in?" is to convene a TEAM DISCOVERY PROCESS with your management. Fortunately, you're the visionary leader of a company that employs a talented team. You're charged with challenging team members to help you achieve your dreams through their assigned roles. When you involve your team, you'll reveal your company's uniqueness as a safe foundation for the future. This all leads to your Optimum Growth Strategy.

Invite your top key managers—perhaps a half a dozen or so— to a get-together. Be sure you include representatives from each discipline: operations, marketing, finance, customer service, product development, quality, personnel, and so on. Your objective? To uncover a composite picture of your business by understanding each person's distinct perspective about your business. This is different from getting one "story" from a single person who, by definition, can only present a picture viewed from his or her own perspective. Obviously, a marketing manager will see your company differently from an operations manager, and so on. But by bringing each of the disciplines together in interaction with each other, a composite picture will be revealed.

> **What does your company do best? What business are you *really* in?**

As you know, multidiscipline groups can sometimes be difficult to work with because each member comes to the table with a different set of experiences and responsibilities.

Such multidiscipline gatherings remind me of the old tale about six blind men describing an elephant. Certainly, the one holding the elephant's tail has a different experience of this huge animal than the one holding the elephant's ear.

Does this story demonstrate how bad it is that everyone has incomplete input based on their limited experience? I don't think so. If you look at these six blind men as managers leading a team, the story takes a different twist. With careful coordination and communication, these blind men actually do come up with an accurate picture! Each reveals a critical detail from his feel of things—a perspective not available to the others.

Similarly, with every member of your management team involved in the get-together, each manager views your company differently. It will be almost like describing several different companies. But when you're careful to capture the common thread, your team has the ability to reveal a magical story about your company's uniqueness—one that might otherwise be taken for granted.

Start with Specific Questions

In this get-together of managers, I use a specific set of questions to involve each of them:

- What are your company's greatest strengths?
- What are your company's greatest weaknesses?
- What market do you serve?
- How would you describe your ideal customer?
- Who are your competitors?
- How do your competitors try to win your ideal customers?

You might be surprised at what your operations person has to say about marketing, or your controller about your ideal customer.

My last question, designed to summarize this Team Discovery Process, is this: What business are you *really* in? Notice that I didn't say what business do you *want* to be in. Rather, what do the *facts* of our Team Discovery Process reveal?

If you thought that this would be a "normal business strategy meeting," you're in for a surprise. In a team environment, creativity flows. Invariably the most unlikely manager comes up with a critical string of words in response to the question: "What business are you *really* in?" Then the others will add to it. Keep the conversation going until you have captured all the Economic Building Blocks the team can find.

Like experiencing a talented Jazz ensemble, people involved in this Team Discovery Process are similar to specialized, talented players who quickly improvise together. Each member takes the opportunity to solo for a while before passing the spotlight to the next player. Then the team unifies in a wonderful common harmony that ties together all the individual themes.

Set A Few Ground Rules

To get the most out of this process, it helps to set ground rules that ensure everyone is understood. Agree to speak the same language—the language of business: dollars and cents. Focus on uncovering the Economic Building Blocks that drive value in your business model.

Here are a few ground rules to help keep your group on track:

- Be sure everyone addresses each question.
- Create a safe environment so people will offer not only what they *know*, but also what they *think*.
- Be prepared to address sensitive issues.
- Don't allow anyone to talk in short hand—for example, don't name a client to explain a problem, leaving participants to come to different interpretations of the issue. Rather, state the problem so that even an outsider can understand it.
- Be prepared to receive some odd feedback from managers who see things differently from how you see them. And, remember, there are no wrong answers. Each answer you glean, however, is an important piece of the puzzle.

In this way, each manager contributes different Economic Building Blocks of your company's uniqueness. Taken together, these building blocks distinctively describe your company in a way that couldn't describe any other company and becomes your company's Competitive Economic Distinction.

Let me share the powerful outcome available from this kind of Team Discovery Process through Dan's experience:

> As you recall, Dan's company automates factory production lines. Its engineers design motion controls that communicate with existing equipment on the factory floor. Dan and his team described their company as a designer of specialized high-tech parts for factory owners serving a small, retrofit market of perhaps $250 million.
>
> At the get-together, the Team's Discovery Process revealed these three key Economic Building Blocks:
>
> - Their motion controllers were imbedded with smart software, making them easy to program.
> - Its electronics division delivered customized parts six to eight weeks faster than any of its competitors.
> - Less than 10% of the company's customers made a repeat purchase within a 12-month period. None of the repeat buyers owned plants; rather, they distributed products.
>
> The team members revealed for themselves that their company was solving the logistical nightmares of customized retrofit engineering faced by distributors. This meant that distributors would gladly buy their simple, programmable solution multiple times a week.
>
> But the real "aha" moment came when Dan and his team discovered that their company delivers customizable solutions to distributors serving a global billion-dollar market with a 90% customer repeat rate.

Now that's a business model shift that's safe enough to build upon!

Here is how Dan explained his experience of the Team Discovery Process:

> *I should preface my remarks by explaining that by the time we commenced Stefania's Team Discovery Process, the management team had been working together for nearly three years at our company. All members had been involved in our industry for at least eight years, and most of us worked together at either of two predecessor employers for several years before coming together.*
>
> *As a group, we had been through many planning sessions, developing mission statements and related strategic planning. I mention this because you would have thought we'd have a reasonably consistent view of the business we're in, the size of the market, and our strategy to penetrate it.*
>
> *Suffice it to say, we didn't. Not because we're stupid or irresponsible, but because we operate in many different segments of a relatively complex industry. Each member of my staff comes to the table with a different set of experiences and responsibilities.*
>
> *The Team Discovery Process, aided by Stefania as an objective outside coach, forced us to simplify our message—not just to potential investors, but to ourselves, to our employees, to our distributors, and to our end users.*

Stefania's process caused us to think more expansively. She helped us remove our self-imposed resource limitations while, at the same time, focused our growth strategy to take advantage of our strengths. 99

Dan

Here's what occurred from my viewpoint:

As facilitator, I was struck by three significant shifts in the team's thinking, all which had important economic ramifications. Each shows how we uncovered Dan's unique Economic Building Blocks.

The first shift had to do with asking, **"What is our market?"** The management team initially calculated the market it served at $250 million. By brainstorming, we uncovered the fact that Dan's company actually served a market that embraced *any* automated production environment. We concluded that their ultimate global market exceeded $4 billion. The significance of that shift alone altered how big a business the team thought they could build.

The second shift had to do with defining the customer. With a dozen people in the room, it was interesting what happened when I asked the question **"Who are our customers?"** A debate ensued over whether they were end users or distributors. The brainstorming process, however, built a consensus around "distributors as customers"—even though the sales team directly dialogued with 95% of its "end users as customers." Knowing this fact is economically critical to Dan's success, since the end user only buys once every decade or so, yet distributors buy every week. Selling to distributors, therefore, affords the company a predictable income stream.

The third shift had to do with the question **"What business are we in?"** The team thought they were in the business of selling "actuators"—a logical conclusion given that 90% of revenue was derived from actuators, the company's only product line for many years. Instead, we highlighted the distinction that this company sells customized *systems* made up of multiple components. This was in contrast to their competitors who sell individual components. Even when it was founded, Dan's company offered an actuator *system*, never just actuator components. This was Dan's value-added approach from the very beginning that the team now took for granted.

Here are Dan's comments:

 As a result of this exercise, our five-year sales growth objective increased from $30 million to $150 million (60% from acquisitions). We redefined our business as providing complete, off-the-shelf, custom solutions to motion control problems (versus individual servo drives, actuators, and motors). We identified our distributors as our true customers (versus end users or machine builders) because that's where the majority of sales are made. We identified our key strengths as our ability to:

* *provide complete, integrated custom systems with short lead times.*

* *rapidly and prolifically develop market-driven products.*

- *Build relationships with our distribution network, allowing us to quickly take advantage of the new products we develop.*

None of this seems like breakthrough stuff. But, for us, it definitely represented a new, more focused way of looking at our business. Left to our own devices, I don't think we would have arrived at that conclusion.

Another unanticipated but welcomed outcome of the process has been the alignment of our senior management team. We entered the process with many different visions of our future and what we had to accomplish to achieve it. We exited with one vision and a common understanding of the path ahead. Interestingly, rather than converge on an 'average' of the group's original expectations (growth rates, revenues, margins, etc.), our collective vision of what we could become exceeded any individual member's original expectation.

Dan

At the opposite end of the spectrum from Dan's high-tech niche-market focus is Greg's company.

In his company, Greg upholsters handcrafted interior trim for the cabs of long-haul trucks—18-wheelers. He urgently needed to increase capacity because this Fortune 500 company was willing to give Greg as much business as his company could handle. When I asked Greg why this was true, he explained matter-of-factly that his team hand upholsters more than 7,000 different parts in multiple colors and fabric combinations, which it delivers "just in time" to the customer's different plants. Over the past three years, they had a defect rate of less than one part per 1,000 despite a double-digit turnover in labor.

Greg's company had already been recognized as a high-quality vendor. This happened because he introduced a high level of professionalism and computerization into an industry where Mom-and-Pop competitors still did their books manually.

Greg and his team considered their company to be a labor-intensive business serving a small niche within the trucking industry. That is, until the Team's Discovery Process revealed a few Economic Building Blocks that were driving value in their business model.

As I asked questions about the Economic Building Blocks that drove value in his marketplace, Greg let his imagination go wild. "If I had capacity," he mused, "I could duplicate my success in the trucking industry in other industries, including the marine, automotive, trains, and buses."

During our brainstorming process, Greg's team revealed the company's prowess in the areas of:

- Distribution logistics
- Customer service
- Worker training

But the real "aha" moment came when they shifted their thinking from "low tech to high touch." Why not serve a billion-dollar interior trim marketplace for trucks *and* autos, buses, boats, and more? The payoff would be realizing much bigger profit margins in this hugely expanded market.

During this process, Greg and his team discovered they were living a tiny fraction of what the future could be. So he converted his thinking about serving the trucking industry, which supported a nice $25 million business plan, into becoming a provider of interiors to the entire transportation industry. This conversion meant building a $100,000,000 business.

At this point, Greg expressed his $100 million-dollar vision not in an apologetic way as before, but with clarity that this vision had become real for him and entire his team. As he said,

66 *This process helped me clarify the most valuable part of our business model. It took me out of the present and into the future.* 99

Greg

For Greg, as with many business owners, it was the first time he had articulated a future that he hadn't dare share with anyone before. The shift happened because of liberating his team's passion about the scope of the vision, combined with Greg's own willingness to put this dream into action.

Can you see how *this* vision will attract serious amounts of money? As a predicable result of the Team Discovery Process, evident in both Greg's and Dan's companies, each team uncovered its unique Competitive Economic Distinction. These motivated managers identified the intersection where value drivers for their customers and the team's own passion brilliantly pointed to what each company does best.

When your entire team gets involved in this Team Discovery Process, each member becomes clear on how he or she can personally drive value in your company; every person buys into the excitement of living this bold vision.

Document Vision-Driven Business Possibilities

Once you gain clarity about your company's uniqueness, you're ready to convert it into action. The next step is to ask your team to translate your unique Competitive Economic Distinction into a set of financial projections. Don't project out just one year or even five years, but project out into the future, revealing what the company is capable of when doing only what it can do best, supported with unlimited resources.

If a typical company's margins look like the "Today" column, then it's not unusual for the team to come up with margins similar to the "Future" column:

	Today	Future
Revenue	100%	100%
Cost of sales	53%	50%
Gross profit	47%	50%
Admin	25%	10%
Selling	20%	15%
EBIT	2%	25%

These are not normal margins—they are *visionary* margins based on your company operating exclusively in its unique domain of Competitive Economic Distinction and supported with abundant resources.

These projections result from capturing all of your opportunities including:

• Successfully penetrating markets and preempting competition.

- Receiving premium prices for innovative new product solutions you introduce.
- Improving margins due to:
  - efficient technology
  - new capacity
  - economies of scale

Together, these all culminate in profit and cash flow cascading to your bottom line.

You'll find that as you and your team draw this picture for your company, an amazing revelation occurs. You'll realize that this growth strategy, based on your company's uniqueness, is much *less risky* than the one you probably would have allowed yourself to pursue *if* constrained by the usual assumptions of limited financial resources.

Your Optimum Growth Strategy, based on your company's uniqueness, delivers the highest return with the lowest risk.

I say that because I believe this is the strategy you'd intuitively come up with if you'd won the lottery! It's the strategy you'd pursue if you had access to all the resources needed to grow as you see fit— to achieve the future you *really* want!

Your Optimum Growth Strategy, based on your company's uniqueness, delivers the highest return with the lowest risk.

True, to accomplish this Optimum Growth Strategy, you'll need funding to get there—perhaps a few million or maybe many millions—but be assured that this strategy has a lot less risk and a much bigger upside than ever.

At $3.5 million in revenue, Greg's EBIT margins were 8%, but at $100 million in revenue, the team projected an EBIT of 21%. These visionary growth margins are based on Greg's company operating exclusively in the realm of what it does best, supported with unlimited resources, as if he'd won the lottery. As he said,

> *I really understand that the future of your business gives it value. If you only have a small future, you have little value.*
>
> *Greg*

But Greg's Optimum Growth Strategy required $10 million—not the $1 million he had originally sought. So how do you get that kind of resource? You need to use your unique currency—your visionary growth—and document it for others to buy. You need to create a Corporate Résumé.

Introducing the Corporate Résumé

To convert this powerful Team Discovery event into a tool, let me show you how to capture your Optimum Growth Strategy as a blueprint to convert your future into action.

I call this tool a *CORPORATE RÉSUMÉ* because, just like a personal résumé, it focuses exclusively on what your company does best.

A Corporate Résumé is typically just two pages long. To create such a succinct description that's easy for non-team Discovery Process participants and even company/industry outsiders to absorb, the Corporate Résumé is written in the language of business—dollars and sense. It looks like this:

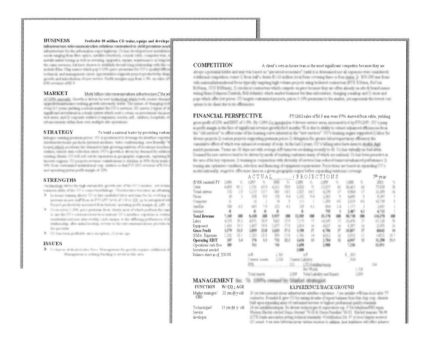

The Corporate Résumé documents your Optimum Growth Strategy converted into financial projections and supported by your unique Economic Building Blocks. These make your revenue and profit margin projections credible.

The financial projections contained in the Corporate Résumé are the ones your team developed assuming unlimited resources. These unconstrained revenue projections are supported by all the required expenses, leaving any deficit to fall to the bottom line and revealing the Timing Gap (before expenses and revenue synchronize) to be financed. Hence, your Corporate Résumé also quantifies the amount of funding required to achieve your company's full potential.

For the best Corporate Résumé product, pull together the best input from your Team Discovery Process. Critical to the success of this process is maintaining objectivity. That's why it's important to use an objective coach to facilitate the process. This coach draws out what you might perceive to be small and insignificant points and perhaps even uncover strengths you didn't acknowledge as such. For the same reasons people find it difficult to write their own curriculum vitae, the coach is better able to summarize the nuggets of information gleaned in the brainstorming session into your Corporate Résumé. These nuggets represent your Economic Building Blocks.

Here's how this worked for Dan's company:

> In my capacity as the objective coach, I documented Dan's Economic Building Blocks that made his company's Competitive Economic Distinction into a two-page anonymous Corporate Résumé. The Résumé included the team's financial projections that quantified their company's growth potential.
>
> As a backdrop, we met at a time when Dan's 12-month sales run rate approached $10 million, returning to the company's 5% pre-tax profitability. Remember, Dan had originally envisioned $30 million in five years, sustaining the company's historic 5% profit margin. In contrast, Dan's Corporate Résumé documented Economic Building Blocks that supported financial projections with aggregate revenue of $150 million during that same five-year period. About $56 million of that was based on internally generated sales (on which Dan projected an enhanced 15% pre-tax profit). He derived the remainder from an acquisition strategy to capture various component manufacturers.
>
> Dan's Optimum Growth Strategy required $2.5 million at a time when his bank had just reduced his credit line. Fortunately, Dan had already learned that vision liberates capital.

As a byproduct, a Corporate Résumé has the ability to harness the creativity of your entire management team in line with your company's Optimum Growth Strategy. Every one of your team members is able to see the same visionary future in no mistaken terms—dollars and cents.

Your Corporate Résumé also closes the gap between what each manager in the company thinks about how to build value. I believe it takes more than open book management to empower your team to greatness. It sets the foundation for Vision-Driven leadership that everyone can follow and execute with confidence—each from his or her own vantage point.

Greg described his results this way:

> *I used to have a vision only as a concept; now I have a vision as a game plan.*
>
> *A concept alone isn't sufficient to motivate my team, plus attract customers and cash. But a game plan empowers us to use our clout.*
>
> *So now I have a dream and an engineer's blueprint.*
>
> *Greg*

To use the Corporate Résumé tool yourself, be sure to work with an objective coach—preferably someone with an excellent dollars-and-cents perspective. While a fellow business owner might be a good choice, avoid selecting anyone who might be tainted by your original (assumption-limited) thinking, such as a fellow CEO in a regular mentor group. I suggest working with an outside businessperson (rather than an advisor such as your lawyer or accountant). In fact, the best coach is a fellow business visionary whose new to your business and has a solid background in finance.

Up to This Point

1. You assessed your current situation by gathering the team to uncover the Economic Building Blocks that drive value for your company.

2. You experienced an "aha" moment after you and your team searched for the answer to the question "What business you are really in?"

3. You converted your Competitive Economic Distinction into a set of financial projections, assuming unlimited resources to reveal your Optimum Growth Strategy.

4. Finally, you documented the financial projections of your Optimum Growth Strategy, supported by the Economic Building Blocks that make the revenue and profit projections credible, using a special Corporate Resume that quantifies your funding requirement.

When you follow this process, you become informed and confident about how easy it will be to achieve your Optimum Growth Strategy and profit from your uniqueness, because you know the secret: *vision liberates capital.*

No one said times are easy, but then for growing companies, times never are. You are always navigating uncharted waters, so why stop now? Growth knows no urgency on its own—only *you* can bring that to the table.

Interestingly enough, today it's easier to get attention for your growth plans than to finance a status quo scenario. Why? In part because the business atmosphere is charged with uncertainty and everyone is searching for a solution. Besides, given the quality of your product/service, shouldn't your company be the market leader? Considering the size of your market, shouldn't your company be a lot bigger than it is? Changing the upside gain your company is targeting can entice a wide range of resources because growth itself is such a valued currency.

As Business Builders, we all have one thing in common: *Our future is bigger than our past because we have the ability to change the future.*

It's Not the Money That's Scarce

I'm here to tell you that YOU, the Business Builder, are the scarce commodity—*not* the money! This is my core message; it's why I wrote this book.

This principle is the source of confidence that supports all the methodologies which make up the Growth Catalyst System. So, don't lose focus of this powerful insight and its glorious significance. Let me say it again; YOU, the Business Builder, are the scarce, most rare and valuable, most precious asset. Once you embrace the full impact of this statement, you can tap into your own wealth at any time.

> **YOU, the Business Builder, are the scarce commodity—*not* the money.**

Perhaps you never thought about it that way before. After all, it's normal to consider what you do *not* have as scarce including traditional resources you never have enough of—resources like money, time, staff, and so on.

It seems like it's easy to forget that Entrepreneurship is not the norm—even in America, the bastion of capitalism!

It's also easy to lose perspective as we operate from deep in the trenches. I remind you again: YOU are the Business Builder. YOU are the source of action who gets things done. YOU are the scarce commodity. It's your energy, drive, innovation, and passion that convert ideas into action. YOU are uniquely able to convert growth potential into profitable reality.

Let me remind you of this: If Entrepreneurship is the business that drives America, then You—the Business Builders—are the heroes of economic life.

Your Vision and Self-Doubt

Here's the biggest question of all: Will you let your business strategy dictate the finance strategy to support it? You have the power of life and death over your company's Optimum Growth Strategy—which is a big responsibly. Will you allow this future to come into existence?

> **YOU, the Business Builder, are uniquely able to convert growth potential into profitable reality.**

The Optimum Growth Strategy is easier to see than do. When Greg and Dan saw their own visions—translated into a set of financial projections and documented in a Corporate Résumé for the first time—all kinds of self-doubts came up. They were really scared.

That's likely true for you, too. It's perfectly human to hear the voice inside your head asking:

- "Can I really do this?"
- "Will our business model really scale?"
- "Do my team and I have what it takes?"
- "Do I even want to think about taking on a challenge like this, even if it were achievable?"

Having clarity about which future is right for you isn't enough. So next, we'll address your fears that the rest of the world won't take your Optimum Growth Strategy seriously.

Chapter 4

Confidence

Addressing the Secret Fears of Building a Big Company

Entrepreneurs are people of action who necessarily take steps before all the details can be worked out. For Business Builders, the same unknowns that entrepreneurs face are bigger and potentially more damaging.

It can be scary to commit to a new path. It takes courage to endure uncertainty. It takes perseverance in the face of criticism from those who don't see the same vision of the future as you do. And it takes a willingness to risk failure and diligently go after your goals. Especially for a Business Builder.

When I addressed the 500 fastest growing companies in America at the Inc. Magazine Gala in Palm Springs, California, in 2003, I was told that two-thirds of the CEOs on any Inc. 500 list averaged two previously unsuccessful businesses before making the list. It seems like the third time is the charm, just like it was for me. (Capital Link is my third and most successful company.)

I don't like the word failure any more than you do, but certainly "learning by doing" is part of the entrepreneurial process. Successful entrepreneurship requires converting challenges into new opportunities. My favorite guru, Peter Drucker, says entrepreneurship is neither a science nor an art—it is a practice. That's certainly true for Business Builders.

Once you have your Optimum Growth Strategy documented in your Corporate Résumé, it's only human to have doubts about your ability to implement and profit from such an ambitious strategy—*even when all the resources you need are available.*

But if you let fear scare you away from grabbing the gold ring, you lose a huge opportunity for your company. But that's not *you*—that's not why you're reading this book. You want meaningful proof to allay any fear that you could damage your company by making uninformed decisions.

This chapter is about a secret fear unique to Business Builders. Discussing your fear openly among employees is taboo because you don't want to appear uncertain with team members who follow your lead. Similarly, you can't appear weak to your peers; you're relying on them to establish and support your credibility. Yet this particular fear needs to be addressed in order to liberate the visionary within you.

Tap into the power of feedback from at-stake, forward thinkers.

Business Builders are sensitive to the inputs that come their way. While there's no shortage of advice, unfortunately most comes from irrelevant sources and has questionable value. It's a natural corollary, then, that their biggest fear is unwittingly damage their companies.

Yet nothing is more powerful than getting feedback from forward thinkers. Better yet, getting feedback from experts who have a stake in your company's success.

The Back Door Approach

I suggest addressing this secret fear of building a big company with a solution called the Back Door Approach. This approach assists you in testing your growth and financing strategy before you commit to it. It also builds your confidence in making decisions about your future while helping you protect what you own today.

Think of knowledge acquired in three stages:

1. You know what you know.
2. You know what you don't know.
3. You don't know what you don't know.

The creation of Dan and Greg's Corporate Résumé relied exclusively on the information they had in-house. Their teams had already dealt with issues they knew about as well as ones they knew they *didn't* know about. So now they need to discover "what they don't know they don't know." How? By extracting objective feedback about their growth strategy. (Clearly, you know far more about your own business than anyone else, but that doesn't mean others can't add new perspectives.)

> **Confident decision-making about your future comes from addressing "what you don't know you don't know."**

Because a Corporate Résumé documents your company's economic distinction, it need not rely on your company name to differentiate it from other companies. That makes a Corporate Résumé a perfectly *anonymous* document to circulate for objective feedback.

That begs the question, "Circulate to whom?" The answer is this: "The smartest investors you can get access to." I like to work with professional investors because, when and if they invest, they're at risk in the same way you're already at risk as an owner. However, before they invest, savvy professional investors become ideal sources of objective feedback. After all, they're in the business of analyzing a company's strengths and weaknesses, which is how they determine where to put their money to work. For a Business Builder, these same factors drive the company's success or failure.

Think of professional growth equity investors as the perfect mirror for your concerns as a Business Builder. Just as you invested equity to create a future that didn't exist when you first founded your company, these professionals invest equity for future benefits. Yet you lack outside perspective because you are *inside* your company, whereas these professionals can objectively evaluate risk and opportunity compared with other deals. They naturally highlight the risk and concerns you would have *only if* you could get on the outside of your company to see it objectively. And when Growth Equity professionals invest, they'll be at stake like you are today.

Conceptually, the Back Door Approach lets you see your growth potential objectively. Said another way, it enables you to test your Optimum Growth Strategy *before* you commit to it, without exposing your company's identification or reputation.

This isn't like circulating a business plan, which is like entering the market through the "Front Door" in an exposed way. Everyone quickly knows your strengths and weaknesses, which can be risky when positive first impressions are critical.

In contrast, the Back Door Approach is designed to be highly educational, insightful, objective, and anonymous. It is *educational* because it focuses on your company's unique potential; *insightful* because it comes from people who have relevant concerns for you to consider; *objective* because multiple sets of eyes yield a market size reaction; *anonymous* so you don't jeopardize your company's reputation. This way, you don't lose the chance to make a "killer" first impression when you do take your refined business strategy to the marketplace!

The Back Door Approach results in the opportunity to:

- Address **business risks** that could sabotage your success *before* committing to a specific growth strategy.

- Uncover **economic factors** that might increase your cost of financing *before* going to a financing source.

- Gain **advance knowledge** about your alternatives in order to make the best-informed choices, with confidence.

- Refine your business strategy to reflect the absolute best your company has to offer the professional private equity and investor community.

Since this Back Door Approach is an anonymous exchange, you get to resolve any issues that could jeopardize your success *before* committing to your vision and *before* exposing your company's reputation in the marketplace.

Remember those Inc. 500 CEOs who failed twice before being included among the most successful fast-growth companies with their third business? I called that practicing in public.

In contrast, the Back Door Approach lets you avoid practicing in public, bypassing the two intermediate disappointments to end up at the final success. So it was with Greg and Dan. The Back Door Approach afforded them an educational tool to make informed decisions with confidence about their future.

> **The Back Door Approach lets you avoid practicing on yourself so you can make a "killer" first impression.**

Because you likely haven't experienced the Back Door Approach, let's rely on the experiences of Greg and Dan to get a feel of what you might accomplish through this approach.

Here is how Greg benefited from the Back Door Approach:

> Greg was excited about his Optimum Growth Strategy, as documented in his Corporate Résumé. But he also felt incredulous. Did he have what it took? Was his strategy finance-able? After all, he had trouble borrowing only $1 million from his existing bank for just a second plant. How would he ever get the money to fund this $10 million, multiplant expansion? Would investors believe in him and his future?
>
> I suggested Greg test his strategy via the Back Door Approach. "Just think how powerful it would be to get experts to help expose weaknesses in your growth strategy that you're too close to see for yourself. Without this kind of objective insight, you might spend lots of time fixing what you think is the problem without addressing other potentially critical issues."
>
> It was my job to select the smartest, most relevant investors possible—all experts in Greg's industry. They would offer their candid reactions on both the company's strengths and weaknesses without ever knowing the company's name. But I questioned if investors who were experts in trucking were the ideal source of feedback. After all, sometimes experts reject novel approaches that challenge their industry-based assumptions. Even growth investors have their biases!
>
> To play it safe, I selected investors from several different vantage points to ensure well-rounded feedback. Of the dozen I chose, a few were logistics experts, some specialized in service businesses (even though Greg's company is a manufacturer) while others focused on general manufacturing. Yes, I did include

several experts in trucking, too. Because of this broad spectrum, the Back Door Approach can provide broad exposure to just the right objective feedback, which I call FINANCIAL MARKET INTELLIGENCE.

I circulated his Corporate Résumé. Within a week— faster than Greg ever thought possible—investors who didn't know who he was shared their candid, insightful feedback about the economics of his strategy.

On the positive side, investors gave Greg credit for his company's:

- Impressive historic growth
- Fortune 500 industry leader customer relationship
- Stunning capacity utilization that generated increasing sales and profit out of a single plant.

On the negative side, investors perceived risks arising from:

- 95% concentration with a single customer
- Highly cyclical nature of the trucking industry
- Growth dependent on labor-intensive plants projected to operate within nine months
- A Chief Operating Officer who was related to Greg, raising questions about his management selection process.

The Financial Market Intelligence that comes from investors must be translated in such a way that Business Builders can respond appropriately. That translation isn't a simple matter of repeating what one hears; rather, it's probing the source, uncovering biases, and accurately analyzing what's being said. Yet, overall, these Investors have the same concerns that you should have. After all, who's already the biggest investor in your company?

> Greg and I explored each issue that the investors highlighted. In our discussions, he revealed many new facts:
>
> - While his company does have a dominant single client, he provided that client with an expanding array of services. Initially, Greg's company had made only upholstered parts. It added just-in-time delivery with complete line-sequencing to demanding requirements at three plant locations, ensuring parts arrived at the right plant for the right chassis at the right time. Next, the company kitted multiple parts for each chassis; then a subassembly of multiple parts from other vendors was added. Greg's people got involved in product design, making it possible to produce parts more cost-effectively. In fact, his company grew from 40% to 60% of his Fortune 500 clients' volume over three years.
>
> - Greg was receiving premium pricing for his company's performance as a preferred provider and was just designated as a single source for all internal trim requirements. This Fortune 500 Company enjoyed their partnership relationship and simply didn't want a second-source backup. In effect, this client depended on Greg, not the reverse.
>
> - While the manufacturing process was labor intensive, even a high turnover rate did not interfere with the company's excellent just-in-time line-sequenced delivery. It experienced a reject rate of less than one part per 1,000

because of excellent training systems that minimized the labor risk.

These were strengths Greg had been missing about his own company and held him back from "selling" his value to investors—or to anyone else, even his customers—until now!

Profiting from the Financial Market Intelligence feedback, Greg integrated the reactions of different investors to strengthen his own strategy. As a result, customer "concentration" became customer "penetration," and a minimum-wage labor force became a "transportable manufacturing process." As Greg responded to each investor issue, he called on his own Business Builder skills to strengthen his plan. He actually heightened his awareness of how to leverage his company's worth. In the process, he became clear about what value he offered clients and how to communicate that to both industry insiders and outsiders for greater profit.

I had designed the Back Door Approach to allow Business Builders to glean critical investor insights affecting valuation and to avoid pricing surprises. Greg also benefited by receiving powerful verification that others understood and valued his vision.

Until now, he had thought he'd have to accept whatever investors offered. Instead, by learning their concerns up front—by finding out what he didn't know he didn't know—Greg resolved issues that otherwise would have cost him more for the capital he was seeking. To his advantage, Greg controlled the outcome by first understanding investor concerns.

Here's a summary of how Greg used the power of the Back Door Approach:

- Investors challenged Greg's business model, given that 95% of the company's volume came from a single Fortune 500 customer. They perceived his model as a simple outsourcing solution subject to severe price competition and annual bidding by a dominant client.

- Stimulated by the investor's objective feedback, Greg revealed these additional eye-popping Economic Building Blocks of his business model:

  - The company was receiving premium prices for its products.

  - His little company was the only supplier *not* to be second-sourced by his major Fortune 500 customer.

  - Greg's engineering team was working with the Fortune 500 company's team to redesign parts to make them easier to produce, package, ship and install.

In response to the investors' concern about customer CONCENTRATION, assuming he was dependent on one customer, Greg realized his business model was based on customer PENETRATION, in which the customer was dependent on him. Through it all, he got clear on how to get more return for the same energy he was already investing.

By the way, these were all things Greg and his team had missed about their own customer relationship. Consequently, they weren't well positioned to profit from these elements of his business model until they became revealed now.

Gleaning Financial Market Intelligence isn't the toughest part about the Back Door Approach. Tougher yet is accurately interpreting it to transform it into a highly educational tool. Using this tool, you can make informed decisions with confidence about both today and tomorrow's growth strategy.

When you want to obtain Financial Market Intelligence for your company, select a translator who has working relationships with more than a handful of investors (perhaps a lawyer, accountant, or financial growth strategist). It would be better yet if your translator had Wall Street experience, even investment banking or venture capital background. Ideally, your translator has his or her own business building experience—a fellow visionary! Be sure that the person you choose can accurately translate raw investor feedback into relevant Financial Market Intelligence. That will position you to take appropriate action on what you hear.

> **Use Financial Market Intelligence to lower the risk of your future.**

Let me tell you how Dan benefited from the Back Door Approach:

> In sharing how Dan benefited from the Back Door Approach, I offer two examples of the kind of statements I heard from investors. They include how I translated those statements into terms Dan could work with and then what he did with what he learned. The investor selection process is very important. For Dan's high-tech company, I wasn't sure if we'd get better input from investors who understood manufacturing or those who understood technology, so I selected a few of each!

Financial Market Intelligence: Example 1: The investors' feedback was that they liked the idea that Dan used "smart electronics" to deliver customized systems.

Here's my translation of what was in their heads: "Customization is, by nature, time-consuming and expensive. Smart electronics might help minimize those expenses a little, but investors need to know how economical it is to scale up. Can Dan's company really build a big company producing customized systems, or will he get bogged down in lots of customer service, with a limited ability to profit from an economy of scale?"

How did Dan use this information? Confronted by this reaction, Dan crystallized for himself the essence of his economic business model. His company's systems are customized at the chip, board, and packaging level, configured from a broad range of pre-engineered parts and subsystems. The company's ability to scale up is driven by the fact that Dan's team can deliver custom solutions right out of inventory. I call this economic model "off the shelf customization." Forced to put this concept into words for outsiders for the first time, Dan strengthened his confidence in the premium prices that this team had forecasted in his Corporate Résumé (which also projected profit margins to rise on the company's internal sales from 5% to 15% pre-tax within five years).

Financial Market Intelligence: Example 2: There was a striking consensus among the investors I polled that revealed a lack of enthusiasm about Dan's intention to acquire component manufacturers. Since the investor challenge was pervasive, I shared the following translation for Dan: "Investors need to know how you will profit more by (a) acquiring seven component manufacturers rather than (b) simply purchasing those components on an as-needed basis as you do today."

Because Dan wasn't in dialogue with the investor source directly, he could take advantage of an unpreserved and tranquil mental space to let this question sink in. "Maybe investors had a valid concern," he thought. Perhaps the acquisition of manufacturers was not a compelling element of his growth strategy. But if not manufacturers, then what else would accelerate his competitive advantage?

Dan revisited our earlier discussions about his close personal relationship with distributors, which he had all but taken for granted—until now. In the motion control industry, distributors are the ones who decide which components an end user will acquire. Dan had spoken about his unusual personal relationship with distributors dating back to his days at his previous employer when he hired engineers out of school to sell motion control components.

However, Dan's former employer's distributors liked the engineers so much that they started stealing the engineers for themselves. Cleverly, Dan responded by offering a program to recruit engineers from school and train them on behalf of his distributors. As a result, Dan personally introduced more than 40% of the motion controls distributors in the entire market to their current profession. From there, Dan drifted away from linking up with other manufacturers. Shifting his attention to a new possibility revolving around the distributors he knew so well, Dan began to think about integrating his unique distributor relationship at an equity level into his Optimum Growth Strategy—a critical decision as you will soon see.

These are just two examples of the objective feedback gleaned from a dozen investors based on circulating Dan's anonymous Corporate Résumé. It only took three weeks, but the impact on Dan's thinking has endured.

Here are Dan's comments:

> *We received valuable feedback and an education about the investor market for our company, all in advance of writing our business plan and without exposing ourselves detrimentally to any of our potential investors. The feedback hasn't changed our business strategy yet, but it definitely influenced how we wrote our business plan and sharpened our growth strategy.*
>
> *While we may not have completely eliminated the various concerns we uncovered from investors, I think we reduced them considerably—certainly enough to get us to the next step of face-to-face meetings with potential investors. We'd have an opportunity to further test our plans—which eventually leads to changing them.*
>
> *Dan*

Vision Revision

When I originally created the Back Door Approach (see the story that follows), I intended to avoid surprises for my clients on investment and valuation issues by providing critically important feedback. Happily, they found this approach equally valuable in testing their growth strategies before they committed to them.

Similarly, the Back Door Approach can help build your confidence based on relevant, real-time Financial Market Intelligence. This process provides the objective lens through which you get to see your company from the outside in. This objectivity powerfully stimulates your own genius to address the business-model weaknesses you might not otherwise notice. It also points out the strengths you take for granted. These factors can depress what you own *today*, because it means you aren't getting full value for what you have, and certainly aren't in a good position to sell in the future.

Dan and Greg each made changes to their business strategy, based on what they learned anonymously through the Back Door, Greg and Dan used the Back Door Approach as a no-risk, low-profile, inexpensive, highly educational tool to resolve or address investor issues before completing their business plan.

Most important, the Back Door Approach provides the opportunity to practice in private, so you don't jeopardize your first market impression. Remember, you'll have many chances to meet investors, but only *one* opportunity to create a first impression. And this market has a long memory!

Dan and Greg refined their growth strategy based on expert input. As a result, they gained the confidence that their:

- future was credible.
- strategy was financially prudent.
- model was financially compelling.
- growth objectives were worthy of sophisticated investor consideration.

And the bonus: they both faced and resolved the secret fears of building a big company!

Life Without the Back Door Approach

You might be thinking, "This approach might work for Greg and Dan, but I don't need it." Well, would you like to know what happens when you don't get expert feedback before exposing your reputation in the investor community? The experience of two of my earliest clients, Henry and Kevin, actually motivated me to develop the Back Door Approach. Here's what happened in their situation many years ago:

The first client was an exciting early-stage company. The company had invented a remote control robot able to perform bridge inspections and detect problems humans can't even get close enough to locate.

The engineer who founded the company, Henry, had done an impressive job. He got friends to help finance the prototype, then won a demonstration contract with the Department of Transportation. He had earned quite a reputation nationwide for his innovative approach to inspection such that he was getting requests to bid on jobs.

Henry came to me to finance a business plan that would introduce a bridge inspection service in which the company owned the robotics equipment that municipal authorities could call upon. Typically, Henry had to perform the inspection once a year. The benefit to the customer was that his company would perform exactly the same robotics inspection each year. Doing this would enable the municipalities to predict rates of deterioration, and allow them to prioritize their scarce maintenance dollars.

To start, I helped Henry design a financing strategy to reduce his need for equity—despite his early-stage status. He would be able to take advantage of the large amount of equipment he could lease, much to his amazement. But I warned him that because his company lacked business management, he needed a CEO.

Henry was quick to agree that even if he were the engineer who could design a racecar, he still needed an expert driver to win the race. However, because he wanted to avoid any delay in going to market for his capital, I accepted his request to simply add his intention to hire a CEO as a use of proceeds. Even though I knew a missing CEO was critical, I felt confident I could find quality investors who would be attracted by Henry's multi-billion dollar market and a service business model capable of yielding a 75% pretax profit margin. I was confident this was a *no-brainer.*

The second company was at the opposite end of the spectrum, with $15 million in sales and a highly experienced management team.

Kevin's company designed and manufactured motor controls, the kind needed to start and stop any industrial production line. But not just simple controls. For example, one of Kevin's customers was a paper mill where the coordination of hundreds of rollers is necessary to spin out wet pulp until it becomes solid paper. Any uneven pull anywhere in the process could break the wet pulp and stop the whole production line at great expense. To date, Kevin and his team had grown exclusively with internal funds. As sophisticated managers as they were, they didn't have experience developing a business plan to support their desire for growth capital: equity. So, they asked for my help. At first, Kevin's team was having trouble writing a plan; it appeared as if his managers didn't think their business offered investors anything particularly distinctive.

I reminded them a lot of companies made hamburgers, but McDonald's stood apart. Then I pointed out the impressive attributes Kevin seemed to be taking for granted:

- A stellar customer list with 95% repeat orders yearly
- A significant penetration in the Japanese market, reflecting excellent quality control
- A ranking just below the market leader in Canada

Kevin incorporated these strengths into his Investor business plan and even added a few charts ranking his company among competitors. But when it came to the financial projections, Kevin was unshakably conservative. After all, he reasoned, he was a CPA himself and had plenty of experience preparing projections. "Yes, however," I explained, "those were the kind you would provide a banker for debt, not a source of equity for growth capital."

Even though the financial projections Kevin developed were conservative, I felt confident investors would see through the numbers, as I did. After all, this client had a track record of beating its own projections!

When I took these two clients to the capital market, lo and behold, we got excellent responses from numerous investors for the business plans of both of these dynamic companies. In short order, we were able to schedule investor visits to both companies. My clients and I were expecting a fast close. *Then the shit hit the fan.*

At the conclusion of the first investor meeting for both Henry's early-stage company and Kevin's established company, we were shocked to learn we had big problems. Concerns about the weaknesses we already knew about raised investors' uncertainty. As that uncertainly increased, so did Henry's and Kevin's cost of capital—much higher than we thought. Plus, the investors I selected based on their industry expertise found more things they were concerned about. In other words, these guys were at risk of losing control of their company for the capital they needed to grow.

While Henry already knew he needed a CEO, he was surprised when investors uncovered that labor unions were fearful of the impact of automated equipment on their job security, and municipalities were nervous about the public finding out the serious status of our infrastructure.

Kevin was shocked that his conservatism backfired. Instead of establishing a floor, as he had intended, investors perceived Kevin's conservatism as a cap on his company's upside. In addition, investors uncovered Kevin's lack of inventory controls—critically necessary to manage the investment he sought. And investors discovered a critical difference of opinion between Kevin and his research and development partner as to which market offered the best growth potential—and direction of how the growth funds were to be invested.

In both cases, as investors continued their line of due diligence questions, Henry and Kevin were surprised to find they really didn't have all the answers. *Turns out they did not know what they did not know, and now it was going to cost them.* At this point in the money-raising process, investors' perception of risk for the robotic company meant funding would cost Henry well in excess of a majority; he would be forced to give up control for capital to grow. The valuation for Kevin's company translated into funding costs approaching a third. In each case, the investors wanted more of the company than either owner wanted to give up. Both of these valuations were much worse than they expected, and devastatingly unacceptable to them and me.

What you don't know you don't know can be very expensive.

Henry and Kevin were sure that the solution would be to find other investors. But I knew differently. These investors they had met were the most knowledgeable investors in their respective fields; others would only have a lesser appreciation for the strengths of these unique companies, causing an even lower valuation for both of them.

A traditional investment banker wouldn't fret at this outcome. After all, an investment banker's job is to let the market set the price. In market terms, this was best price either of these companies could get, *given the risks the investors had identified.*

For me, as an entrepreneurial investment banker, though, this outcome was definitely not good enough. Remember, I started life as an entrepreneur and Capital Link is my third company. I knew in my heart and mind this outcome didn't reflect the full potential of these companies. This experience led me to create the Back Door Approach as a way for clients to educate themselves about how to drive value.

This is what got me thinking: "If only I could figure

out a way to let Business Builders see for themselves what I could see, then we could team up to alter the outcome."

The ideal scenario would be to get investors to offer their candid reactions on both strengths and weakness, but without really knowing who the company is, to preserve a clear shot at a "killer" first impression! But how? By introducing the company incognito—perhaps under an alias. Think about the benefits that would give Business Builders—a way to learn about any investor concerns before identifying themselves. Well, no company with integrity would do such a mischievous thing, but I developed the next best thing.

I leveraged working relationships with investors willing to review "no name" profiles and offer these companies the candid market feedback they desperately need before formally entering the market under their own names. By knowing investor concerns up front, Business Builders would have the choice of resolving these issues or accepting that they'll have to pay for them with equity.

The result would be the best deal possible because the company wouldn't be penalized by any weakness it undertook to resolve. Years ago, I named this my Back Door Approach because it lets Business Builders see a company through investors' eyes without jeopardizing the opportunity to create the best possible, dynamite first impression. And it has been working ever since.

Luckily, what happened to Henry and Kevin need never happen to you. Through this Back Door Approach, you have a solution to the Business Builder's secret fear of building a Big Company.

Control

Creating an Investor Who Shares Your Vision and Wants You in Control

Most people think a direct trade off exists between equity and ownership. That is, the more equity *funding* you seek, the more ownership *control* you will have to give up. They believe that acquiring $5 million of equity funding requires giving up more ownership than if they acquire $1 million equity funding—an assumption that stems from a huge self-limiting belief.

Actually, the reverse is true. Typically, the more growth capital your vision can justify, the more ownership you will retain—and that ownership will be worth a lot more, too! That's why I say **Vision Attracts Capital.**

_____

Jack created this chart as a way to prove to himself that the more funding he seeks, the less ownership he gives up.

The chart indicates that by raising $5 million of equity in 2004, Jack's majority ownership is almost twice the value it would be if he were to accept only $2 million of equity. That's true even after paying investors three times their investment in 2009, which is five years later.

That is the power of fully funding his Optimum Growth Strategy. Instead of Jack's ownership being $13 million (of $19 million Company Value), it's $22.5 million (of $37.5 million Company Value).

Jack's Chart: the Power of Funding the Optimum Growth Strategy

2004	2009 Results			2009 Ownership Analysis				
Capital Investment	2009 Revenue	EBITDA $	% of Rev	Enterprises Value	2009 Debts	Net Enterprise Value	Investor's Value	Company's Value
No new capital (10% Growth)	$27M	$2.7M	10%	$13.5M	$1M	$12.5M	$0	$12.5M
$2M new capital (15% Growth)	$33M	$4M	12%	$20M	$1M	$19M	$6M	$13M
$5M new capital (22% Growth)	$53M	$7.5M	14%	$37.5M	$0	$37.5M	$15M	$22.5M

Assumptions:
Enterprises Value - 5 x $EBITDA
Inverstor's Value = 3 x $new capital invested
Company's Value = Net Enterprise Value - Investor's Value

The Power of Professional Equity

Your Optimum Growth Strategy deserves to attract smart Professional Equity. As a Business Builder, you owe it to yourself to examine this option closely.

Here are secrets I've learned as a Business Builder on the "inside" of the financial community:

- When your business strategy dictates your funding strategy, you, not the investors, are in control.
- The *right* investor is created, not *found*.
- Getting the highest valuation is not only a good idea; it is imperative.
- Management having majority equity ownership is critical for a growth company.

These suggestions I offer from my years advising Business Builders:

- Never divert your attention from building the value you want to sell to investors. That goes for your team, also. Regard raising equity as a specialized job, not a side job for you, your CFO, your account-ant, your lawyer, or your management team—you get the picture!

- There is (dumb) money and there is *smart* money. Dumb is just cash; smart has the ability to understand your business, make introductions, and accelerate your progress. It's a non-cash component of equity money.

> **Your Optimum Growth Strategy deserves smart Professional Equity.**

- If you want (dumb) money, you do a lot of talking—in other words, you make pitches for it. Dumb money also costs more while it yields less support for your future than smart money does.

- If you want *smart* money, you do a lot more listen-ing. Smart money sees the wisdom of your Optimum Growth Strategy and wants to not only ride the wave of your success, but support you in every way it can.

- No one can speak and listen at the same time; this is where an advocate comes in.

- It takes an experienced industry player to shepherd your deal and assure quality attention for your story. With deals coming at them from all directions, investors can get overwhelmed. An entrepreneur might have no market credibility *per se,* but can gain instant credibility when partnered with a seasoned advocate.

- Because investors and entrepreneurs don't always speak the same language, you need to work with a talented translator.

Certainly you have learned a great many things during your career. I trust that ideas in this book have added to your wisdom—including how to use the Mosaic Approach to attract abundant resources and keep control of your company.

Raising money is your responsibility— not your job!

However, if it's time to access Professional Equity, reading this book isn't enough. Please don't try doing this on your own. Raising money is your responsibility—not your job. You deserve an Advocate to help you do it.

Raising equity is a full-time job and you already have one! This is no time to divert your attention from building the value you intend to show investors. Successfully getting financing is a reflection of a well-run business—never the reverse. So, use the rule of comparative advantage. Add a professional to your team. But not just any investment banker will do. A typical investment banker raises capital based on the present value of a company while a true Advocate takes on a much bigger role than that. Beyond empowering clients to make their future value tangible for the financial community to buy, your Advocate selects investors attracted to your biggest possible future. That translates into the highest valuation—and a relationship in which you keep control.

Raising equity is a full-time job and you already have one!

Use an Advocate as Your Growth Coach

Once you've selected an Advocate, take advantage of that person's role as your coach. Just as you spend time recruiting, interviewing, and hiring just the right manager to join your team, sourcing the right capital partner for the right growth strategy warrants the same meticulous process. This is where a coaching relationship can be especially valuable.

A professional coach knows the game and how to position the

players to WIN. A coach for growing companies focuses on:

1. Selecting the best equity partner to finance the optimum strategy to achieve your full potential.

2. Lowering the cost of that capital.

3. Providing strategies and years of experience so you can WIN the game.

4. Lending personal connections in the capital market to secure preliminary Financial Market Intelligence.

5. Positioning you for the best deal.

6. Ensuring that you use your power to determine what percent of equity you'll share with investors.

> **Growth challenges you to build a team dedicated to what your company can be.**

As a bonus, a good growth coach helps you unlock your full potential and answer the question: "Imagine what your company could look like in five years if you were operating at capacity today, with no cash constraints."

Remember, growth flourishes where there are believers and challenges you to build a team dedicated to what your company can be.

Equity—Your Cheapest Form of Funding

Here's an opportunity to test my statement that "when your future is dramatically bigger than your past, equity can be your cheapest form of growth funding."

Chapter 2 explained that professional equity investors invest in private companies such as yours to earn a higher return than their clients can earn in the traditional public markets.[1] These profession-

---

1 *The Professional Equity market is made of professionals who invest as a full-time job. You could think of professional investors as "portfolio managers" managing the capital of their clients, insurance companies, and pension funds, whose investment dollars are held in committed ten-year partnerships. See Chapter 2.*

al investors are attracted to bold plans. They completely understand that their success of achieving higher returns for their clients' money depends on your success. Of course, creating a successful match requires knowing how to locate the right investor for you.

Who is the Right Investor for YOU?

When you decide to focus on the Professional Equity market, you get to select among more than 2,000 investor partnerships that manage this multi-hundred-billion-dollar marketplace. Selecting the right one can be confusing because not all committed growth equity is the same.

The right investor not only offers abundant resources, but also shares your vision and comes with a commitment to help you get where you want to go. This investor wants you in control.

How do you find this right investor? You don't—you need to *create* the right investor for you. You share your own vision and personal goals. You share your Optimum Growth Strategy, the one you'd pursue if you had access to all the resources needed to grow your company. You share the financial projections developed by your team based on doing only what your company does best. After all, if you don't tell the world where you want to go, how can anyone help you get where you really can go?

The right investor *wants* you in control.

The Front Door Approach

Up to now, you've learned about the Back Door Approach that has preserved anonymity for your company—an approach designed exclusively for your edification. However, once you've gone through it, you're well positioned to proceed to the market through the Front Door. The *FRONT DOOR APPROACH* is when you meet investors face to face. Based on peer relationships that you create, you'll uncover the right investor for you.

The Front Door Approach is made up of these seven elements:

- **The Valuation Maximizer**—*The Investor Business Plan*

- **The Investor Self-Selection Process**—*Selecting Investor Choices*

- **Getting a Ph.D. in Your Own Business**—*Face-to-Face Meetings*

- **Team Empowerment**—*Inviting Investors to Meet Your Team*

- **Capturing the Outlier Investor**—*Getting the Term Sheet*

- **Checking for the Smartest Money**—*Doing Due Diligence on the Investor*

- **Creating the Right Investor for YOU**—*Getting the Highest Valuation*

Here's how Dan accessed the Professional Equity marketplace through the Front Door Approach and created the right investor for his company.

1. The Valuation Maximizer—The Investor Business Plan

Dan developed an Investor Business Plan that was short and concise. His plan was just 12 pages of text that expanded the content of his Corporate Résumé by addressing all the investor concerns revealed via the Back Door and incorporating the strengths he had previously taken for granted. It also included historic financials, and, most important, detailed projections of Dan's Optimum Growth Strategy, including full assumptions that quantified his funding requirement at $2.5 million. It is important to make the distinction that the Optimum Growth Strategy is not the most aggressive set of projections, nor the most conservative; but it's not the most probable either. It is simply the projections you would finance if all the money needed was yours.

There are many kinds of business plans and they aren't all alike. Some are designed for internal audiences like your team (perhaps for your operations or marketing manager); others are designed for external audiences (perhaps for your banker). As you can imagine, each of these plans might dictate different kinds of projections. Clearly, an investor business plan isn't like any plans noted above.

Never include a valuation in an investor business plan; that represents a ceiling, not a floor.

The purpose of an investor business plan is simple: to educate investors using economic justification to support your visionary future. Most important, in this investor business plan, no valuation should be mentioned. That would represent a ceiling, certainly not a floor. Besides, the market determines the valuation; it's your job to educate the market to get the value you deserve.

2. **The Investor Self-Selection Process—Selecting Fund and Investor Choices**

With your Investor Business Plan in hand, you need to decide with whom to share it. Choosing investors is based on several parameters. Some are related to the company, such as Dan's industry, stage, and rate of growth. Some are related to the investors, like their risk appetite, exit horizon, areas of business expertise, and location. All growth investors have their own risk-taking biases, so it's important to start with investor candidates that fit basic parameters.

Many entrepreneurs who seek growth capital go to the wrong investors and don't realize that the rejection they receive has more to do with the investors than it does with them. A typical professional growth investor receives more than 1,000 business plans a year, most of which do not meet their investment parameters. They typically respond to about 150 of them, mostly those that are "sponsored" as opposed to those that come in "over the transom," as we say in the industry. Ultimately, such professional growth investors only meet face to face with a few dozen entrepreneurs a year.

Rejections have more to do with the investors than it does about the entrepreneurs.

Because the right investor is created, not found, I prefer to let investors "self select." Investors are attracted to your vision, so circulating your Corporate Résumé via the Back Door Approach helps determine which "type" of investor will give you the best reception for the value you have to offer.

In Greg's case, I discovered the best reception came from those investors with expertise in logistics and services (surprisingly, not in trucking and manufacturing). So I carefully sought more investors who had investment characteristics that emphasized those areas.

For Dan, I discovered the best reception was investors on the east coast who liked Dan's blend of high tech but low risk due to the basic industries that made up Dan's motion controller clients. This contrasted with west coast investors who perceived his technology as "not techy enough." Consequently, I sought a broader mix of non-west coast technology investors.

I extrapolated from all this information to identify 30 interested investors, each well suited for Dan's business and vision. That's 30 out of a possible base of over 2000 private equity funds. I wanted to ensure that Dan would have choices.

It was my job to circulate Dan's Investor Business Plan to the right general partner within each of these 30 Professional Equity funds. This methodical selection process ensured that with just 30 plans in the market of more than 2,000 investor partnerships, Dan would have a balanced market introduction. I suggest never shopping your deal with too many Investor Business Plans floating around in the marketplace. (In this "clubby" marketplace, investors like to office in the same building like the famous venture capital office building on Sand Hill Road in Menlo Park, California, eat at the same chi-chi restaurants, and go to the same Starbucks.)

Next, I followed up by telephone with each investor who received a plan so I could evaluate the reaction to Dan's vision and goals. Out of this pre-screening process, I scheduled 13 investor meetings for Dan in eight states over a two-week period. (For Greg it was nine investors in five states over a one and half week time frame.) Why so many meetings and so close together? Because I want to:

- create time urgency for investors! Orchestrated parallel meetings put time on our side.
- position Dan to make informed decisions. I call this getting a Ph.D. in your own business.

3. Getting a Ph.D. in Your Own Business—Face-to-Face Meetings

With each investor meeting, Dan set out to educate investors about his business while, at the same time, testing his economic model against rigorous (yet benevolent) investors' analyses.

Dan shared a similar presentation with each investor. Yet he was surprised how differently each investor responded to the risks and opportunities in his business. Dan was discovering that value is not objective—it is a matter of perception.

Just as his team members saw the company differently during the Team Discovery Process, so did each of these investors. Dan learned a lot. I believe the opportunity to have this kind investor exchange is the single most significant learning experience an entrepreneur can have—like earning a Ph.D. in your own business.

> **Value is *not* objective—it is a matter of perception.**

What Dan learned from the Ph.D. program at U of M—The University of the Marketplace:

I went into the process to learn about the capital raise process. We did that. What I didn't expect—and what was at least equally as valuable—was to learn as much as I did about my own business. Nothing in my experience has been so effective at honing a business strategy as having to describe and defend it to a series of seasoned professional equity investors.

Dan

What Greg learned from the University of the Marketplace:

I have read a lot of business books about business philosophy, but I didn't really have any anyone to talk with about these concepts until I met these professional investors. A dialogue with these investors is just like the language in the best business books. But here it is live, applied to my own company.

From day to day, I focus at the operational level. I think about expansion. Now I realize this expansion thinking is only at the conceptual level. The details of how to actually implement this growth for my company isn't clear. Yet I didn't worry because that expansion is in the 'future,' not today.

This interaction with professional investors allowed me to get clear about the critical ingredients needed to move my company's future into the present. I realized I have to prepare now to get to the future I want. During the investors' exchange, I got the benefit of many important questions which stimulated

*my thinking about what I needed to do opera-
tionally, not conceptually.* 🙲

Greg

4. Team Empowerment—Inviting Investors to Meet Your Team

Next, we invited selected investors back to visit the company's plant/office to meet the team. Just as I had prepared Dan and Greg to meet with investors, I now coached each team member to get and give the most out of each investor exchange. Their involvement became key because all investors know it takes a coordinated team to carry the ball over the finish line.

The more inclusive this investor meeting process is, the faster the investor decision-making process goes. This is also extremely empowering to the team members who have been coached to understand the importance of their role in deepening the perception of value, which investors want to buy. Investors are buying management's execution talent—so present the entire team to demonstrate all the critical skill sets required to get the job done.

5. Capturing the Outlier Investor—Getting the Term Sheet

Most owners want to have Term Sheets in hand as quickly as they can get them. But they don't realize they are pushing for something that doesn't serve them. Doesn't it make sense that the earlier the Term Sheet arrives, the more it will have risk premiums depressing the valuation? Conversely, the later we get it, the more time we have for both of us to understand each other and the opportunity. Once a good investor relationship is created during personal interaction, the contents of the Term Sheet won't be a surprise: All the terms will have been spoken out, discussed, and understood—the why's and how's. The Term Sheet is the last thing we want because it contains the valuation.

Dan was delighted to receive five Term Sheets. What surprised him most was not that each had different terms and conditions, but that there were *five different valuations*. The highest was almost *double* the lowest. True, markets are generally efficient, with most investment offers clustered in a tight range. But statistically, there will always be an outlier—the one investor who offers the largest number of dollars for the lowest percent of your company based on a deep understanding of the business opportunity and the skills you bring to profit from it.

> **Dan received 5 Term Sheets with 5 different valuations; the highest was almost double the lowest.**

Best of all, Dan realized he was totally *in control* of creating his own outlier investor. All he had to do was educate the investors. You see, the Professional Equity market relies on one-on-one dialogue to establish value. This means that your passion and vision become a valuable currency in dialogue with professional investors. When you and your team describe your future credibly enough for these investors to buy, you can get credit for that future *today*.

Dan was about to benefit from THE POWER OF NEGO-TIATED VALUE in which the smartest, most knowledgeable professional investor establishes the value of a company based on the owner's vision and unique ability to implement the optimum strategy.

Negotiated Value is an important concept and merits explaining it in more detail.

The Power of Negotiated Value is getting credit for your future *today!*

Negotiated value means you can get credit *today* for the value of your future *tomorrow*. That's compelling for a Business Builder like you because your company's *present* value is only a fraction of what its *future* value could be.

Let's say your company earns $1 million today, but you project earnings of $5 million in three to five years. We'll select a Price/Earning ratio of 12. This means an assessed value of $12 million gives consideration only to your past ($1 million of earnings times the 12 P/E) while a value of $60 million today gives consideration to your future ($5 million earning times the 12 P/E).

Say you need $1.2 million to finance the growth program that gets you to $5 million. You have three choices. You can:

1. Sell 10% to an investor who sees only your past.

2. Bootstrap your business and take five or seven years, not three, to grow it. Meanwhile, your competitors could be catching up or moving ahead of you.

3. Seek investment money from someone who shares your vision of the future and will give you credit for it today.

The $1.2 million in the third option requires something at the 2% end of the range of ownership give-up, rather than the 10% end of range:

10% _____ 2%

Present Value   Negotiated Value

When you make your future tangible enough for investors to buy, you'll receive credit for your management skills and see movement on this spectrum.

Fortunately, the Professional Equity market offers you the opportunity to take advantage of capital sources attracted by your power to create value. This means you get to influence the value outcome.

The Power of Negotiated Value is derived from a basic tenet of the capital markets: **value is not objective.** This tenet is known to professionals who work in the market, but perhaps it's not fully appreciated by those outside of it. It isn't derived from intrinsic value. In fact, there's no such thing as intrinsic value. If there were, both buyers and sellers wouldn't willingly be exchanging stock at the same price in the market every day.

Making the future tangible enough for investors to buy is management's job.

Value is a matter of perception. This concept was introduced with the Mosaic Approach *but it's rarely used to its full potential.* Perception is so powerful that it has been known to change presumably objective facts. Did you ever see an accident at an intersection? Honest people stand firm that they're reporting facts objectively. Yet a pedestrian explains the accident from one vantage point and the two drivers involved have stories that don't match. The policeman reporting the incident gets overwhelmed with conflicting data. So it is with equity. That's why, in the capital markets, **value creation is management's job.** Fortunately, the Professional Equity market is prepared to pay up once you've educated it.

For a discussion of Valuation and ROI, see **Appendix A:** *Valuation: It's Not Just About ROI.*

6.   Checking for the Smartest Money— Due Diligence on the Investor

With a value for his company established, Dan could focus on which investor was right for him. All money has personality, some of it valuable and some not. Specifically, Dan focused on the non-monetary elements that are a critical part of any investor package.

Dan did his own due diligence on the investors. He asked for the names of several portfolio CEOs from each investor candidate and asked three questions of each CEO:

1. How did this investor team react when things went better than expected?
2. How did this investor team react when things went worse than expected?
3. What talent sets and contacts did the investor bring to the CEO's table?

Dan learned a lot from the portfolio CEOs and his thinking evolved along the way. This increased his confidence to proceed with his investor selection process.

More about Dan's Ph.D. program at the University of the Marketplace:

> *Face to face meetings that Stefania arranged revealed that investors were generally impressed with the relationship I had with the distributor network; one way or another, they thought there was something there of value that could be leveraged. However, most investors leaned toward a strategy of serial acquisitions of man-ufacturers, because it appeared to be a natural extension of our business plan, and because my experience was all with manufacturers.*

> *I, for a number of reasons, was beginning to lean in the direction of concentrating exclusively on the distribution element of the M&A strategy, doing what I was uniquely positioned to do: attracting the initial critical mass necessary for our growth engine.*

> *My leaning became a decision following a piv-otal meeting with a senior partner at one of the investment firms under consideration. This is a premier professional equity firm, second largest in the world. The guy I met is in charge of all their North American investments. His com-ments essentially were, 'The manufacturer roll up makes sense, but I think the amalgamation of distributors might be more leverageable and could take greater advantage of your unique skills. A combination with distributors appears*

to offer more opportunities for synergism, and the growth potential is nearly unlimited.'

I was impressed with this gentleman's vision, primarily because he agreed with me. Joking aside, it was helpful to me, as I was struggling with this decision, to have someone with this level of experience and reputation—with his investment perspectives—confirm the viability of a strategy that even my own staff was seriously questioning. It was great to have someone of this caliber on my side!

At the end of the day, we received five Term Sheets from professional investors all proposing to invest in my company. The one with the highest valuation came from this gentleman's firm. Stefania reminded me that it's not unusual that the firm you're most attracted to is the one that gives you the highest valuation. The people in that firm most closely share your vision and see the value in what you're trying to accomplish.

Dan

At this point, Dan was ready to take my suggestion of creating an investor syndicate. Even though each Term Sheet offered all the money required for the current plan, Dan liked the idea of multiple, deep-pocketed investors in the current round to be better prepared for both unexpected opportunities as well as unpredictable challenges.

7. **Creating the Right Investor for YOU—Getting the Highest Valuation**

Dan selected two of the five investors he liked best. Instead of accepting any of the Five Terms sheets, we created a sixth one and included the best terms and conditions and highest valuation from the ones we had received.

Not surprisingly, Dan invited the investor who had come in with the top valuation—one of the investors he'd taken a liking to. (It's not unusual that the investor you like the best will come up with the highest valuation. Value, like beauty, is in the eye of the beholder.)

> **We created our own Term Sheet, selecting the best terms and highest valuation of those we had received.**

Interestingly, Dan also invited a feisty Professional Equity investor who had asked thought-provoking questions but who had been one of the lower bidders. Dan thought he would contribute rigor to the team. But it took a rigorous dialogue between Dan and this second investor to resolve that investor's perception of risks. After their conversation, the second investor reconsidered his initial valuation and agreed to come up to the top valuation of our sixth Term Sheet.

Details of Dan's Success

In short order, Dan accepted $2.5 million for 26% of his company. Was it worth it? Yes, because Dan achieved his ten-year revenue dream in just one year. As you know, Dan's company grew from $10 million to $100 million in just one year from receiving his funding. He did it by converting that powerful distributor relationship into an entirely new distribution channel. **Plus, Dan accepted two more rounds of follow-on funding[2] effortlessly from the same two investors, at valuations exceeding five times the original investment just two years prior.**

> *The process we went through with Stefania is one that I believe has broad applicability and cannot help but result in bolder, more exciting, and more wealth-enhancing plans.*
>
> *I expected to raise the $2 to $3 million I thought I needed to optimally promote and support the products we had developed in order to build a $25-30 million company in five years. I expected to do this at a reasonable valuation while retaining control.*
>
> *I got that, but, also a lot more!*
>
> *I realized a better understanding of my own business:*
>
> *What was unique about it.*
>
> *What was of real value to our customers.*
>
> *What was of value to investors.*
>
> *What was leverageable.*

---

2 *Whether milestones are met ahead of or behind schedule, growing companies always need follow-on financing. A critical attribute of accessing professional investors is that as soon as they make an initial investment, these experienced growth managers typically set aside a reserve for follow-on investment—often equal to or even exceeding the initial sum invested. They've already anticipated your future growth needs. Remember, the dollars used to finance your growth are* NOT *discretionary dollars—you know, those elusive dollars that family, friends, and angels have one day and don't have the next. In contrast, Professional Equity partnerships are self-contained capital sources. Their deep pockets are the result of a ten-year structure designed to accommodate the realities of a multi-year business plan with committed resources.*

> *I also got very 'smart money.' Not just capital,*
> *but the expertise and business contacts which*
> *these investment companies represent as well as*
> *two new outstanding board members.*
>
> *Ultimately, I uncovered an entirely new growth*
> *strategy from the one I originally envisioned,*
> *one that has already resulted in a business that*
> *is $100 million just one year from our closing*
> *with these investors. We will be public by the*
> *end of next year and I am completely confident*
> *we will grow to over $1 billion in seven to eight*
> *years.*
>
> *Dan*

Timeline for Dan's Success

March 13	Stefania acted as objective coach for Dan's Brainstorming Session. Two weeks later, Dan's Corporate Résumé was completed.
April 18	Dan authorizes circulation of his anonymous Corporate Résumé.
May 8	Dan and Stefania glean Financial Market Intelligence from 12 investors within three weeks.
	For four weeks, Stefania and Dan integrate investor feedback into the business plan.
June 7	Dan's business plan is circulated to waiting investors.
July 9 - Sept. 13	Thirteen face-to-face investor meetings occur in eight states.

September 3   Stefania introduces Brain Trust manager[3] Steve to Dan.

September 12 - December 12 – Steve and Dan "beta test" a new relationship.

October 25   Dan's Board considers five Term Sheets and selects two premier institutional investors.

November and December - Investor due diligence and deal documentation.

December 31   Closing: Dan accepts $2.5 million for internal growth plus $1 million for shareholder liquidity.

February 28   Dan invites Steve to join his team as VP General Council.

October 29   Dan's Board approves merger with 12 distributors.

December 1   Dan projects sales of $100 million.

Here's what Dan says about his Brain Trust Manager:

> *Amalgamating or merging 12 businesses at one time has a number of legal, SEC, and tax challenges to it. If I had been using our law firm to do this, it would have easily been a $500,000 bill. I could never have come up with the structure that was as creative—and favored our shareholders—as well as this one has. My Brain Trust Manager Steve has been an incredible strategic help. Again, I didn't really know I needed this*

3 Dan did not have on board the full staff necessary to build his new business. But neither did he know exactly what talent he should be looking for to help him achieve his vision. His Brain Trust manager Steve not only had practiced law, but had been a vice president and investor in a company he helped take public several years earlier. Steve was looking for a new opportunity where he could invest his unique skills.

person and if I knew I needed this person, I wouldn't have had a clue as to where to look. Stefania introduced us and we put Steve on a three-month retainer (Stefania called this a "Beta test" relationship) to help us when we were closing the investment deal so we got a chance to work together for a couple of months. Now, Steve is a very, very, very key member of the team and he came for basically some stock options. He took a 50% cut in pay to come on board because he knew the value we could bring to each other and he's gotten some stock options. You know he had to believe that this thing was going to $100 million or he wouldn't have done this. He has a vested interest in the outcome and he'll make out very, very well as a result of his 'investment' for which I paid not a dime.

Dan

Details of Greg's Success

Not only did Greg have a choice of all the money he wanted, but Greg also got to choose among important non-monetary attributes available to support his goals. Greg selected a Midwest Institutional Investor. He liked the personality match between John, the manager of the fund, and himself. He felt John understood and respected his plan, and was investing in Greg's ability to execute a vision they both shared. In fact, the investors were really "great guys," not at all like the investors entrepreneurs hear about and fear are out to replace the company owners.

Greg's investors were prepared to be a sounding

board for his ideas and challenge him, then offer their contacts and the resources he needed to enhance his strengths. Greg's investor unlocked numerous doors and supported him in multiple ways. John's next-door neighbor was the Director of the State Department of Development, which was convenient considering Greg wanted to open a new plant in that state. Two of the largest banks in the state were pension investors in the fund and every single state pension program was a major investor so introductions for debt funding were no problem! In short, this particular investor had more to offer than Greg ever imagined possible.

To address a deadline to get extra business from his Fortune 500 customer, Greg needed to open his first new plant. These investors dropped what they were doing because of the value Greg's business plan had to them. They were prepared to stick their neck out for him before completing their due diligence. John put $1.5 million of equity into Greg's pocket as a bridge loan, which triggered a vital banking relationship and liberated cost-effective state funds aggregating $7.3 million.

Greg discovered the power of smart, professional investors who supported his biggest ambition. They offered introductions and helped leverage his equity and theirs. Because they were selected based on a shared vision, his investors wound up being "hands off," trusting Greg to accomplish their shared goals. Best of all, his investors offered the emotional support and professionalism to position Greg to grow his company into the one he really wanted.

Greg did not just assume these attributes. He verified them through his own due diligence by speaking with

each of the investor's portfolio companies and com-
paring the input he got directly and indirectly with his
other investor choices. (It's easy to know you have the
best deal when you have alternatives to choose from.)

Greg was confident of his decision—he closed the deal
with this investor and had $3.1 million of equity in his
bank account in ten weeks flat, leveraged by $7.3 mil-
lion in low-cost bank and state funds to minimize his
equity give up while funding his full $10.4 million
multi-plant expansion plan. Plus, his investor's deep
pockets enabled the fund to set aside an additional $3
million in follow-on reserve capital to accommodate
opportunistic acquisitions—another growth phase or
just in case "a wheel fell off Greg's cart."

**Greg thought he would have to accept what was
offered. He did not expect speed, much less choice,
and he certainly did not expect to have the opportunity to negotiate.**

*It's important to understand we, the entrepre-
neurs, set the terms of the deal. We take it or we
don't—not the investors. They make offers, but
we accept or counter them. We sign up only
when we are ready. We are not at their mercy.*

Greg

Timeline for Greg's Success

June 20	Greg and Stefania met for the first time.
	Seven days later, Greg's Corporate Résumé was complete.
July 5	Anonymous Corporate Résumé is circulated.
	One week later, Investor intelligence gleaned from back-door feedback.
	One-month vacation—Greg takes a break!
	Two weeks Stefania assists Greg with integrating market feedback to sharpen growth strategy.
September 15	Business plan completed and circulated to awaiting investors.
October 3-12	Nine Investor meetings occur.
October 7	First meeting with final choice investor.
November 14	Greg accepts $1.5 million from the investor to meet a client imposed deadline and $7 million bank and state funding is received.
November 2	Stefania introduces Brain Trust manager Tom[4] to Greg.

---

4 *Greg took advantage of a Brain Trust Manager with 28 years of profit and loss responsibility. This former general manager of a $400 million General Motors division had opened numerous plants in the U.S., Europe, and Pacific Rim. Greg might never have sought a manager of this caliber, but Greg was certainly willing to talk when Tom approached him. As a result of this proactive selection process, not only benefited from a safety net of experience but he gained high level industry contacts in a new market he wanted to penetrate.*

Greg's vision had already been expanded by his Back Door feedback but Tom's 28 year hindsight fueled Greg's vision with ideas Greg could not have had based on his own experience. Within hours, Tom was downloading knowledge, expertise, contacts and more. Tom saw Greg's company as a platform he knew he could build on.

Tom's value to Greg was driven by the fact that he didn't want what Greg already had. Rather, he only expected and wanted to share in the creation of a future that didn't exist. What a great deal for Greg! For every dollar of new value he shared with Tom, Greg kept $7.

One week later they meet; Tom's expertise allows Greg to see an even bigger vision.

December 31   Due diligence and deal documentation consummated with his Investor.

Fiscal Year End 12/31   Greg completes year with $7.8 million in sales.

January 1   Tom is on board.

January 31   Greg's company is generating $21.6 million annualized sales out of its single plant.

June 30   Four plants operational; Greg's annualized revenue exceeds $25 million.

Getting the highest valuation is imperative.

High Valuation Confirms a Good Choice

In the final analysis, securing the highest valuation is not just a good idea; it is imperative. Receiving the highest valuation becomes your mathematical confirmation that you have adequately educated your investors.

Perhaps pale in comparison, $3 million of patient equity in exchange for 25% of his company allowed Greg to attract the resources he needed to grow his $3.5 million company. It turned a respectable 8% EBIT profit margin into a $25 million company, generating a much more impressive 15% EBIT profit margin *in just one year's time*. Greg set his company on a path to achieve quantum growth and profit when he let his vision attract capital.

When asked what would have happened if he had gotten the original $1 million he had sought from his bank to fund his initial business plan, Greg said:

It would have been a nice, but small business, doing $25 million with no knowledge of the phenomenal opportunity I had left on the table. Getting turned down for that $1 million opened the doors to a future I didn't know I could have. Why didn't I do this earlier? Why do it at all? Am I really ready for the full potential of my dream? I was scared to death. Even though we were the industry leader at $7.8 million in sales, I was afraid to ride the wave of that success and tell people about the potential I could see. I was afraid of embarrassment, not having all the answers, and of being boastful. I was afraid of sharing information with bankers, managers and most of all with investors who would not share my vision and would divert attention from my goal. I was afraid of sharing ownership. Afraid of the expense required by the process of growing, I had heard stories of 'vulture capital' and how friends had embarked on capital raises that went nowhere. Above all, I was afraid to admit I was not going to get any further without outside help. These were all scary issues only because I didn't know enough about them to address my fears.

It has been a long, interesting, educational, and rewarding journey. When I started it, I had no idea this is where I'd eventually end up. It is a much better place than the one to which I was originally heading.

Greg

The future both Dan and Greg are now pursuing is safer, more profitable, and more competitively distinctive than the one either had previously considered—or even imagined!

You know, Dan never thought of himself as a "Business Visionary" until he realized he was one! So it was with Greg too. I invite you to make the same discovery about yourself and your team. By

YOU, the Visionary Business Builder— not financing— are the scarce commodity.

understanding the process they went through, I hope you can see how you can take advantage of this process for yourself.

A properly designed financing process yields valuable market intelligence to stimulate your own unique genius PLUS the resources you need to execute. Cash and Control—you can have both!

Right now, billions of uninvested committed dollars are burning a hole in the collective portfolio pocket of the Professional Equity investor community. It's your decision, now that you know that YOU, the Business Visionary—*not* the financing—are the scarce commodity.

Imagine what you could achieve if capital issues were not a limitation. The next step is yours!

Now is the time to let your vision liberate all the resources (human and capital) necessary to achieve your Optimum Growth Strategy.

That leaves the logical question: Are you taking advantage of your clout as a Business Visionary?

Transformation

Sustaining Vision-Drive Growth

It's your future, so choose the one you want. *It is all about mind over market.* Let me explain.

Conventional thinking says growth is dictated by the market-place—by the customers. Therefore, most people define traditional growth as finding a fast-growing market, jumping in, and following its trajectory.

Luckily, Business Builders aren't restricted to that reactive thinking process. Entrepreneurs have access to what I call *PROACTIVE GROWTH*.

Proactive Growth is when you identify a problem, innovate a solution, and design your own Optimizing Growth Strategy. This differs from traditional growth, which is highly risky. In traditional growth, you cope with all kinds of risk factors imposed from the outside and

What will you choose—traditional growth or Proactive Growth?

beyond your control. Today's volatile and uncertain economy makes this reactive mode seem overwhelming and exhausting.

In contrast, Proactive Growth actually takes advantage of dynamic market changes as fuel. Built on what you do best, it leverages your natural strengths so your biggest risk is *opportunity loss.*

Now, you won't have absolute control, but a sure way to lower the risk of your next growth stage on a path toward sustaining Vision-Driven Growth is to grow proactively.

Here's an example. I've always been fascinated with what I perceive to be the transformation of the sneaker industry, also called "athletic footwear." A few decades ago, no one would say that gym shoes were a hot growth opportunity. In fact, the other day, I saw a woman wearing a flat canvas lace-up shoe and thought to myself, "That looks really uncomfortable!"

Well, Nike made the same observation in 1972. They identified the problem of comfort for people active in everyday sports. Nike experimented with waffle-bottom designs used by the competitive sports professionals and introduced cushioned, comfort "sneakers" for the consuming public. But it did not stop with one shoe for *all*. Rather, Nike created one shoe for *each*: a shoe for basketball, a shoe for jogging, another for cross training, and more. Now, the company even makes fashionable athletic footwear.

Do you remember when a pair of sneakers cost $9.95? Today a pair of Nikes costs $120—and that's the sale price. While Nike capitalized on Proactive Growth strategies, KEDS, a brand-name company in the sneaker marketplace, succumbed to the risks of traditional growth. Yet, Nike's ambitious growth strategy wasn't risky for this innovative company laser-focused on "sport foot comfort." Nike's Proactive Growth has been rewarded with leading a transformed market. Even as new entrants follow, Nike keeps innovating and profiting from its unique understanding of a market it created. Best of all, this kind of Proactive Growth positions a company to access a new and exponentially higher level of business performance.

Proactive Growth positions you for *sustained profit* over time. You just might have more control over your future than you thought. After all, it's your future so you can choose the one you want.

Vision-Driven Growth is an Innovative Process

Running your company is not a job; it is a passion! Enjoy it and keep it fun for you and your team. Together, you want to make a difference in the world, not just work for the sake of work. That's good news because the challenge of a growth company is to keep growing, to innovate again and again. Need I remind you that if you are not growing, everything you've already invested is at risk?

Vision-Driven Growth is a process. So when you focus your entire team on the factors that drive value for your customers, you establish a culture of Business Builders inside your organization. Doing that sets up your company for Vision-Driven Growth.

That requires inviting feedback from your team regularly. For example, Dan and Greg use different kinds of Team Discovery Processes throughout the year. Each likes to name his process: one calls his quarterly check in **THE VISION PROTECTION PROCESS** and the annual process **THE FUTURE UPDATE**; the other has a monthly **VISION ON-TRACK PROCESS** and a remote site retreat called the **VISION REVISION**. Find your own ways to nurture the art of Business-Building within your organization. (You can start by sharing this book with your team.)

> **Vision-Driven Growth is a process.**

In contrast to systematic Business-Building team meetings, many companies make the mistake of thinking of growth as a *transaction* (typically associated with a capital raise) instead of a process. Growth is not a matter of waiting for the right economy or other external factors to come along. Properly nourished with market possibilities and financial intelligence from this methodical, predictable Growth Catalyst System, your company will continue to raise barriers to entry, escalate premium prices, achieve salability, and protect huge markets. That's how you can liberate the visionary Business Builder within you. That's how you tap into the "passion profits" of your most robust business model.

Now you know the elixir: Growth can be self-funding when you use your own currency! Did you ever stop to think that growth is a continuous series of start-ups and Timing Gaps? Prudent Business Builders don't start big; they take on the introduction of each growth spurt as they did when they started the company. If you are introducing a new product line or expanding into a new market, each is a "start-up" of its own—testing your reception on a small, beta scale. For the start-up phase in developing a new product or service, investment from family and friends will suffice for a small safety net—perhaps up to $100,000. When you're ready for initial market introduction, you can capitalize on funds from Angels. They offer their personal industry expertise to quantify market unknowns and provide a cheap source of funding until you demonstrate true market acceptance. Then, when you are at the commercialization phase of your newest growth spurt and need a few million for national or even global market rollout—and you need it at a speed sufficient enough to protect crucial market penetration—seek out deep pocket Professional equity. Anything else would be RISKY, and you'd add financial risk to your basic business risk.

Without an adequate equity safety net, you add financial risk to basic business risk.

Now you have a template for funding sustainable, high performance growth.

Sustain Vision-Driven Growth with Liquidity Planning

Even though growth is the lifeblood of a sustainable company, diversity of risk is often a required stimulus so you can go to bat again and again. Innovation and growth have its risks. When you began your company, it was easy to take the gamble because you had less at risk relative to a huge upside. However, as you've grown, you have built a net worth and personal obligations. Having a concentration of your net worth in your growth company causes a prudent Business Builder to be more cautious with each new "risk-taking" investment. Past success can insidiously cause a company's future growth and appetite for new ideas to slow down.

To avoid this dilemma, it's appropriate to take partial liquidity for yourself along the way. Indeed, it's healthy for you to take a few marbles off the table at successive growth stages. This is in sharp contrast to what too many Business Builders do; they sell out because of insufficient resources to grow just before the biggest payoff is achieved. Diversifying your personal investment concentration in the company invariably reinvigorates the life-sustaining, risk-taking innovation your company is built on. Call on the "personal liquidity planning" attribute of the Professional Private Equity market as a powerful growth stimulant. The winner is *you*, the Business Builder, because you're in control of your perpetual profit-making machine.

> **Diversifying your investments reinvigorates the life-sustaining innovation your company must build on.**

Let's face it, a fundamental reason for creating value is to eventually have something worth cashing in. Everyone wants a path to liquidity, just like investors do. Planning a liquidity strategy[1] is part of being an informed Business Builder—whether you're selling some, all, or none of your equity or just planning your future. The logical approach is to work with experts.

Professional Equity investors are experts at maximizing returns on their investment—and *yours*. It's a perfect division of

---

1 *Going public is not the only liquidity strategy available. Even for investors, an IPO is often not the preferred liquidity event. Neither is selling the entire company. Other alternatives include selling the investor's minority stake to a strategic player or buying back the investment made by investors. In an environment of low interest rates, banks are happy to lend against the appreciated value you have created and finance a "Recap" (recapitalization). That lets you use bank debt to buy out an investor's stake. Because you have several options, don't allow worries about how to exit prevent you from bringing in professional capital when you need it.*

labor. Once you and the investor select mutually acceptable liquidity options, you focus your activities *internally* to ensure the success of the company. At the same time, professional investors focus *externally* on the capital markets to identify key timing considerations.

Vision-Driven Growth Yields Transformational Economics

Success over changing economic conditions demands that you innovate *systematically*, especially during the good times. Only in this way you can be ready when the markets change, as you know they will.

It's your innovation that drives Proactive Growth. Naturally your Optimum Growth Strategy logically results from capturing your best opportunities and building on your company's unique Competitive Economic Distinction. When you allow yourself to fund and implement your Optimum Growth Strategy, you unleash THE POWER OF TRANSFORMATIONAL ECONOMICS: sustainable, extraordinary business performance unique to you, capable of attracting abundant resources while preserving control.

Let me share these three predictable results of Transformational Economics for your company:

1. **Exponentially higher profit** by harnessing the energy you're *already* investing

2. **Dramatically lower risk,** as you accelerate growth *built upon your unique strengths*

3. **Enhanced shareholder wealth** as you maintain control over your destiny, even in the face of a volatile economy

Transformational Economics is built on these practical, yet transformational principles:

- YOU, the Business Builder—not funding—are the scarce commodity.
- Growth is your own unique currency.
- Vision attracts capital.
- Cash and Control: You Can Have Both
- You *can* control the future.

YOU, the Business Builder, are the most advanced species on the planet.

By leveraging these first principles, you'll notice the most important take-away from this book is this:

- **YOU, the Business Builder, are the most advanced species on the planet.**

  You create value.

  You excel under uncertainty.

  You profit from change.

  You thrive where others can't even survive!

It might be scary to think about this, but you know that others in the world have come to depend on YOU—the Business Builder. That is why I say you are the most advanced species on the planet.

Based on the confidence you've gained from Principle #1 (YOU, the Business Builder—not funding—are the scarce commodity) empowered by Principle #2 (Growth is your own unique currency), you operate from the stance

Business Building visionaries like you are in demand!

that your Business Strategy dictates your Finance Strategy, never the reverse.

I invite you to harness your own genius and commit to action Principle #3 (Vision Attracts Capital). When you let Vision Attract Capital, you profit from the synergy of all these Transformational Economic principles.

I cringe at the thought that lacking these insights (and experiencing what almost happened to Jack, Greg, and Dan) would relegate *you* to remain a relatively small business—a business filled with all the pain and none of the profit of your true passion. But now that you know the secrets of self-sufficiency that build value, attract resources, and preserve control, the choice about *which* future you really want is YOURS.

Your reward will be sustained Profitable Growth. Faster. Safer!

Your Reward is Sustainable Profitable Growth. Faster. Safer!

The resources are out there for the boldest plans you can think of. Liberate your most ambitions dream. Visionary Business Builders like you are in demand.

Since you're going to invest the time, energy, and intellectual capital anyway, the idea of getting the highest ROI by pursuing your Optimum Growth Strategy is a great one. The time to do it is now.

You get the *Cash*; you keep *Control*. Your future calls! Are you ready?

Appendix A

Appendix A: Valuation: It's Not Just About ROI

Valuation and ROI are big focal points of Business Builders seeking professional capital for the first time.

To get a new perspective, let's put ourselves in the investors' shoes for a moment.

Now that we've selected the one deal out of 100 opportunities we're prepared to invest in, it's time to cut a deal.

How do we investors decide what ownership of the company we want in exchange for our investment? Before we can answer that question, we need to reflect on the rules of the game.

We each have $100 million to invest and are competing with each other to win. The only way to win is to have the most dollars at the end of ten years. In investor language, that is to earn the highest Return on Investment (ROI).

What exactly is ROI—return on investment? And how does it effect our investment decision?

Return on Investment is a calculation comprised of three components, all summed into one number:

1. How many dollars went out?

2. For how long?

3. For what return?

It's a useful calculation because it takes into consideration time and its cost. Time is a key consideration for every equity investor. Unlike debt, which accumulates interest daily, equity seeks capital appreciation. Equity reaps its return only at the end, if at all. ROI is objective and mathematical because it's calculated after the fact.

ROI is really a marriage between what an *entrepreneur* can do and what an *investor* can finance.

As investors, we have no way to demand a return on investment, only a way to nurture the entrepreneur who can create a return for us. So, if you think about it, the job of...

the entrepreneur is to:	**the investor is to:**
manage resources	nurture entrepreneurs with resources

Successful investors understand that the entrepreneur is the one who actually creates value. But we are two different people looking at the same opportunity, each from our own perspective. So it's not surprising that our *goals* are different. The goal of…

an entrepreneur is to:	**an investor is to:**
operate a $100 million company profitably, no cash flow problems.	get five times the money in three years generating 71% ROI.

To achieve these two different goals, it's not surprising that each of us is *focused* in different places:

The entrepreneur is looking at getting money *today*.

The investor is looking at getting a return in the *future*.

Appendix A

Too often, entrepreneurs let themselves focus on getting money *today* as the end of the process. In reality, it's the beginning.

Let's step back and see how, as an investor, we can enhance our ROI. We'll start with considering the three components of ROI:

Component 1: How much do we invest?

Mathematically, the fewer dollars we invest to achieve a set result, the greater our return on the investment will be. However, the biggest mistake investors and entrepreneurs alike can make is to put too little capital into a deal. Insufficient capital offers just enough for now, assuming everything goes right. But the future is unknown; we could lose our total investment if we don't plan for uncertainty.

The first thing any serious growth investor will do is set aside a reserve. Typically, a reserve is an amount equal to the original investment.

Some entrepreneurs sabotage themselves, unwittingly, by asking for too little money—perhaps because they fear giving up too much equity, or because they think a smaller amount of money is easier to get. Whatever the reason, it's our job as investors to ensure that the entrepreneur has educated us fully and that we really understand the total picture.

> **Some entrepreneurs sabotage themselves by asking for too little money.**

As investors, we want to finance the Optimum Business Strategy because that's the one with the lowest risk and highest return. The better we understand what the entrepreneur really needs, the better positioned we are to help with all our contacts as part of a value-building team approach.

Component 2: For how long?

From our investors' perspective, we know we only have a ten-year investment life. We must liquefy all investments by year ten to calculate our ROI and see who "won." But time is relevant well before year ten. Let's look at how significant timing is to our ROI:

If we can make three times the money in three years, our ROI is 44%. But if it takes two years longer, three times our money only equals 25% in five years.

To see how significant time is to an equity investor's return, notice that $1 of investment that returns $3 in three years earns a respectable 44% ROI, but if that same $3 takes five years to come back, that same investor only earns 25% ROI. A $1 investment that returns $5 in three years earns a ROI of 71%, but if it takes seven years, the ROI drops to 26%, comparable to only receiving $3 in five years.

Dollars Out	For How Long	Dollars In	ROI
$1	3 years	$3	44%
$1	5 years	$3	25%
$1	3 years	$5	71%
$1	7 years	$5	26%

That explains why, as equity investors, we "aim" for higher ROIs in deals that have longer planned exits, such as start-ups. It shouldn't be surprising that, going in, investors "target" 50+% for early stage deals with their seven- to ten-year time horizons, 35-50% on second stage deals with their five- to seven-year time horizons and 25-35% for later stage investments with their three- to five-year time horizons.

In summary, the bigger the risk (or longer the length of time for a return), the bigger the required ROI. Start-up investments demand a higher ROI than do LBO investments.

However, no matter what investors "targets" going in, ROI is calculated based on how long it took and how much came back, if anything.

In reality, out of a portfolio of 30 deals over a ten-year period, we'll likely end up with a few write-offs, a lot of sideways deals, and, if we are lucky, a super-star or two. To win the game, ROI is calculated on a portfolio basis.

Whatever our ROI targets are in the future, how-ever, our daily goal is to support our entrepreneurs with whatever it takes: contacts, money, knowledge, and feedback to reach our shared growth goals as fast as possible.

Why? Because if we don't exceed 25% ROI in our portfolio per year, we could have done better buying art or trading stock on the public exchanges rather than taking the business risks inherent in growing enterprises.

Component 3: What do we get for our investment?

Together with the entrepreneur, we get to select mutually acceptable exit options. As investors, our key responsibility then is the timing of those exit alternatives, based on market conditions.

It's a natural division of labor for management to focus internally on the success of the company and for investors to focus externally on the capital markets. This works well because we both want the same thing: the biggest, fastest return possible—the best ROI!

As we can see, ROI is a useful calculation for investors to compare against each other and determine who won the game. ROI is mathematical and objective; it can be because ROI is a resultant calculated after the fact. It's a great way to keep score.

But ROI can't tell us how to calculate how much equity we should ask for in exchange for our investment up front. We still don't have an answer!

So, if investors can't use ROI to determine what percent of the company we want in exchange for our investment, what can we use?

Easy. The only valuation tool that exists is the present relationship!

That should not be too surprising, once you realize we already know entrepreneurial talent alone is not enough. (Otherwise you wouldn't be here reading about how to find investors.) And neither are dollars alone sufficient. (Or investors would not be coming to me looking for you!)

Relationship is the only valuation tool that can incorporate the unique combination of assets. It takes a specific entrepreneurial team and a specific investor team to create a future in which the whole is greater than the sum of the parts. It's just like a marriage!

On day one of the investment, any discussion of ROI targets still happens in fantasyland, yet to be created by the right team and the passage of time. Here we are today. Unlike ROI, which is objective, the percentage is a subjective decision. Negotiating what percent of the company an investment deserves is the beginning of a five- to seven-year partnership.

Chances are, each of us could get comfortable with a different percent as our share in a fast growth company in which we felt comfortable with the management. That's normal.

True, statistically, most of us would cluster in a small range, but there will be a loner, a maverick investor, an outlier. An outlier is the one investor who will offer the largest number of dollars for the lowest percent of his company—all based on relationship.

Let's go back to being the Business Builders we are. Every entrepreneur always wants the largest number of dollars for the lowest percent give up, what we call "the best deal."

The best investor relationship will translate into the best deal for you.

Unfortunately, too few entrepreneurs realize this is *totally* within your control.

All it takes is for you to find the investor with whom you are the most comfortable: *That best relationship will mathematically show up as the best deal.*

Notice that the percentage of your company given up in exchange for the capital of an investor is not dictated by the size of investment, nor the stage of growth, nor the industry, nor anything objective for that matter.

The best deal is simply evidence that you have

found the dream investor who shares your vision and is committed to help you achieve it.

And, by the way, this relationship is the one that offers your company its greatest prospects for ultimate success. A good marriage is heaven; a bad one is—

Just as you have spent a lot of time recruiting, interviewing, and hiring just the right manager to grow your business, investigating your ideal capital partners deserves the same careful selection process.

Now is no time to leave things to chance. That's where a professional comes in, as *your* advocate. Your company and your dreams of the future deserve success.

Acknowledgment

Each insight in this book is the result of teaming up with a particular Business Builder willing to explore their greatest corporate ambitions. It is an honor to acknowledge the many clients who have contributed to the essence of this book:

Joe Abraham, David Alexander, Eddie Allbright, Andrew Bachmann, Brad Baiocchi, Ernie Baker, Fred Baker, Charles Ballantyne, Mark Bayer, Bernie Benson, Jamshed Bhathena, Martha Bidez, Dr. David Black, Evan Bull, Jeff Buratto, Kevin Busch, Greg Cauterucci, Bob Clements, Michael Dommenge, John Dennan, James Eatrides, Denise Fugo, Will Geddes, George Gersema, Jeff Glickman, Elliot Goldman, Jim Griffin, Michael Gualario, Daniel Halpern, Dick Hejmanowski, Walter Herbst, Rob Hoover, Elizabeth Hubbard, Lyric Hughes, Stephen Hutchinson, Scott Johnson, Jay Koch, Gary Koerner, Carl Kutsmode, Richard Larkin, Jonathan Lau, Jean Ledieu, Dan Limbach, Glenn Lombardi, Bob Machesic, Wayne McFarland, Robert McGuire, Phillip McKinney, Kyle McQueen, Marilyn Miglin, Frank Milligan, Tom Mohrhauser, Peter Morris, Mike Motta, Doug Mow, Peter Muzzy, Dr. John Nelson, David Newberger,

Denny Ogden, Okokon Okon III, Denis Oudard, Randall Over-field, Randy Partin, Sanjay Patel, Orazio Pater, Mark Petersen, Morris Pettit, Ann Price, Douglas Ranalli, Randall Maddox, Daniel Randolph, Choppy Rheinfrank, Lansdon Robbin, Mark Rosenwald, Michael Rouse, Michael Santucci, Jason Saul, Pat Scala, Dan Schnaars, Mark Schwartz, Darren Schwartz, Curt Sharp, Mike Silverman, Alden Snyder, Chris Sorensen, Severin Sorensen, Jack Staton, Michael Stickney, Dominic Stramaglia, Alan Swift, Paul Tenczar, David van der Merwe, Sam Van Land-ingham, Greg Verderber, Paul Vragel, John Walker, Nicholas Weingarten, Elliot Weissbluth, Bruce Weitzman, Thom Welling-ton, Ken Womack, Dr. Ioannis Yannas.

A special acknowledgment is due to Wayne McFarland and Scott Johnson. I have had the privilege of working with each of these Business Builders in several of their different companies as their growth ambitions have been manifested. Wayne and Scott have each joined me at the podium of several national CEO con-ferences, generously sharing their experiences. Their willingness to share has allowed me to address what is really inside the Busi-ness Builder's head as one confronts the "business visionary growth adventure." I am fortunate to have them as clients (who have repeatedly tested the process), as excellent communicators, as believers that this process should be shared, and most espe-cially as friends. In particular, Wayne volunteered to edit my manuscript, taking time away from his own pressing deadlines. I am deeply and personally indebted to Wayne for his insights, counsel, passion, and unfailing commitment in meeting chal-lenging timelines. To bring this book to life, I value the client and professional input of my beta readers who, in addition to Wayne and Scott, included Bernie Benson, Jonathan Lau, Dan Limbach, John Sabl, and Dan Schnaars.

For years, the messages compiled into this book were devel-oped as speeches. I thank my speaking coach Kathy Brown for her guidance on how best to communicate to my special audiences. My favorite speaking venture for this message is the Inc. Magazine conference where, for over ten years, I had the honor to address CEOs. Thanks to former Conference Coordinator Brain Murphy and, more recently, to Senior Content Manager Gina Imperato, who believed in my content. I wish to also acknowledge the editorial leadership of Inc.'s founding editor George Gendron and current editor John Koten.

I would not have started this book had it not been for the enthusiastic urging of Barbara Hemphill and Dan Sullivan. Guidance and how-to came from the many powerful connections through the National Speakers Association and the generous giving professionals associated with it. I am indebted to Cyndi Maxey, president of NSA-Illinois in 2002 (the year I was inducted into the organization) and current president Kevin O'Connor, its Illinois and National staff, my Master Mind Group Polly Jensen, Randi Killian, Diane Wilson, and Nina Barrett. Special thanks to Greg Godek who helped give my book shape and form.

Thanks to my friends at Particulare Press whose efficiency made this project fun: Barbara Mitchell, Jim Patterson, and a team of specialists including my literary lawyer Lloyd Jassin, book designer Mary-Lynne Bohn, and editor Barbara McNichol.

A writer needs a special kind of place to write, and nourishment too, for which I am indebted to the gracious proprietors and patient staff at Wolfgang Puck's at the Museum of Contemporary Art, and Einstein Bros. at Rush and Walton, both in Chicago. They afforded me food and shelter for the many hours it took to finish this manuscript.

Sourcing the intellectual and emotional stimulation that preceded this work, I acknowledge the University of Chicago Graduate School of Business both as my alma mater and for sponsoring my Mind Your Own Business program to advance the study of Business Builder issues. Special thanks to Former Dean John P. Gould, Dean Edward A. Snyder, Caroline Karr, and the entire GSB operational teams. My practical wisdom was vastly enhanced by my former employers "Herbie" D. Levine and John E. Dancewicz. I owe a deep debt of gratitude to Cynthia Harringon for expanding my definition of possibilities and to Walter Peters at Life Spring. I could not have done without the emotional nurturing and mentorship of my husband James M. Condon, as well as my sisters Carly List and Leslie Aulicino; my advocates Elfrena Foord and Kathy Graham, and of course my parents, Mary and Armand Aulicino.

About the Author

From Stefania Aulicino: Passion in Action

I was the "idea" partner in my first company that I founded right out of college in 1972, and I had a "money" partner. Our first client sent me to Paris on assignment. After a few weeks of being there, I telexed my partner to send more money. The response I got went something like this: "no further funds to follow . . . fend for yourself." That's how I learned a fundamental truth about entrepreneurship: *Access to capital is the lifeblood of any growing company.*

That day, I vowed never to be hostage to capital again. And the day after, I decided to go to Wall Street to study the business of finance from the inside out. In the process, I learned something else—something that almost no one else knows how to do. I learned how to build value and keep ownership control—the secret of self-sufficiency. This secret is so valuable, in fact, that I decided to share it with fellow entrepreneurs through Capital Link, a company I founded in 1988. (Please take a complete tour of our company at www.CapitalLinkUSA.com.)

As The Entrepreneur's Advocate

In my capacity as The Entrepreneur's Advocate, I've had the privilege of partnering with the CEOs of hundreds of privately owned companies with revenues ranging from $3 million to $50 million in high-tech, low-tech, and service industries. Using The Growth Catalyst System to convert their growth potential into profitable reality, I have raised more than $125 million in professional equity for them. In every situation, the owners have retained control in their firms.

I assist my clients in achieving exponentially higher profits, dramatically lowering risks, and enhancing shareholder wealth. In the process, I stimulate the thinking of many entrepreneurs to uncover the Business Builder within.

Mind Your Own Business

MYOB is a learning laboratory for CEOs scaling up their companies to their next growth level.

In 1982, I created—and have since directed—a program for CEOs called Mind Your Own Business (MYOB), which is sponsored by my alma mater, the University of Chicago Graduate School of Business.

MYOB is a learning laboratory for hundreds of CEOs who strive to take their companies to their next level of growth. MYOB is available to the entire community of Business Builders, regardless of university or industry affiliation.

The structured interaction I facilitate through MYOB is based on two distinct premises:

- CEOs learn best from like-minded Business Builders—forward-thinking, at-stake peers—not from outside speakers.

- Business Builders learn faster hearing about the *successes* of their peers rather than discussing others' *failures*. And this kind of learning is so much more fun, too!

I believe that Business Builders like you deserve an objective, nurturing, supportive place to go—allowing you time to open your mind to new possibilities for your company's future.

Allow me to extend a personal invitation to join your peers at MYOB, where the topic is always your company's profitable growth. Please check the MYOB calendar for meetings times on the Capital Link website at www.CapitalLinkUSA.com.

As a Speaker-Educator

Over the years, I have addressed national groups of CEOs that have included the Inc. 500, TEC, YEO, YPO, and the Council of Growing Companies to share my innovative methodology. My passion is to show business people in my audiences how to create higher returns on the energy they're already expending to build their companies.

My programs provide Finance, Growth and Leadership solutions to groups of privately held companies seeking profitable growth. They can be presented as keynotes, half-day seminars, full-day workshops, or two-day retreats. Participants have said, "Stefania is an inspirational keynoter. Her seminars are strictly bottom-line; her workshops are consultative; her retreats are truly transformational."

As a Sailor and Dancer

The only way I know how to relax from building my business is exploring other passions that (temporarily) focus my attention away from the work I love.

One-design sailboat racing with our local Rhodes 19 fleet does it for me on Sundays and Wednesdays, plus competing in national events around the country when we can. With 12 to 15 boats on the starting line for regular races and 30 to 40 boats at a national regatta, it takes all the strategy and team leadership skills I can muster to get optimum advantage from the wind, crew, and nautical maneuvers. It's similar to navigating a company through a competitive landscape. My husband, Jim, shares my passion (we met sail boat racing and our wedding cake even had two little boats on top as a substitute for bride and groom figures!). And competitive sailing attracts other business owners—just like me!

Jim (my husband of 18 years) and I also love ballroom dancing. Besides taking regular classes in Swing—East and West Coast versions, Foxtrot, Latin, Argentine Tango, and Waltz, we enjoy our "salad course" dancing. We're often the first couple on the dance floor when the orchestra strikes up at charitable events. We're not great dancers; we just love taking any opportunity to improve a move or two!

Service Marks

The following are Service Marks of Capital Link and Capital Link USA:

The Entrepreneur's Advocate
Cash And Control: You Can Have Both
The Growth Catalyst System
The Growth Catalyst
Business Builders
Vision-Driven Growth
The Front Door Approach
The Back Door Approach
Competitive Economic Distinction
Economic Building Blocks
Corporate Resume
Financial Market Intelligence
The Vision Gap
The Timing Gap

Team Discovery Process
Negotiated Value
Mosaic Approach
The Brain Trust
The Entrepreneur's Catalyst
Optimum Growth Strategy
Proactive Growth
Passion Profits
The Vision Protection Process
The Future Update
Vision On-Track Process
Vision Revision
Transformational Economics
Capital Link practical yet transformational principals:
YOU, the Business Builder—Not Funding—
    are the Scarce Commodity.
YOU, the Business Builder:
    The Most Advanced Species on the Planet.
Growth is Your Own Unique Currency.
Vision Attracts Capital.
Cash And Control: You Can Have Both
You can control the future!

Index